Don't Get Snowed

Don't Get Snowed

A Guide to Cross-Country Travel

by Michael J. Riley

Greatlakes Living Press, Publishers, Matteson, Illinois

Greatlakes Living Press
21750 Main Street
Matteson, Illinois 60443

CONTENTS

To the members of my family, both natural and
adopted, especially to Victoria

Foreword

Thirty years ago Alpine, or downhill skiing, was a sport limited to a few ski areas and a hard core of individualists. They presented themselves at the foot of the lifts armed with wooden skis, bear trap bindings, clunky boots and bamboo poles. The most stylish ski attire was the heaviest, most bulky sweater you could lay your hands on.

Remote as this scene may be from the one which would greet you at the modern alpine ski areas, there is one important similarity. Even in the earlier days of Alpine skiing the sport developed in well organized ski areas. Ski patrolmen were present for safety and if a skier became cold or tired, there was the lodge at the base of the hill. The average skier did not have to pack his lunch and extra clothing in a pack that he carried onto the slopes. There was little reason for him to learn the technical side of avalanches or first aid, because there were experts at hand to cope with these emergencies. If the weather suddenly turned bad, you simply stopped skiing and sat it out in the lodge.

In this country we are experiencing a restlessness. There seems to be a need to turn away from the city, the organized and the structure — to escape into nature and draw from within oneself for freedom and solitude. So it is with skiing. Nordic, or cross country, skiing is growing by leaps and bounds. People who have never before ventured beyond the protective limits of their cities are spending their winters in the mountains and wood, lands.

Unlike the Alpine skier, who has the protection of the skiing community, the Nordic skier is left on his own to handle emergencies.

To develop all forms of skiing while providing a safe and enjoyable environment for all skiers, the United States Ski Association (USSA) began early to develop a training program for the Nordic skier. The association's objective was to furnish a mechanism for the skier to obtain back woods knowledge to survive in his new environment. This training program became known as the White Diamond Course. The USSA drew upon some of the most knowledgable people in the field when organizing the program. The course is now being taught across the country under the auspices of the USSA in what is probably the finest and most well-rounded program for the safety of skiers.

This book was born out of a need for a text for the White Diamond Course. It includes many suggestions from experts in the various fields covered in the book. *Don't Get Snowed* and the White Diamond Program are not designed to present Nordic skiers with a set of hard rules, but to give them the freedom that can come only when they have a good concept of their winter wilderness environment. The freedom to reach beyond the protective limits of society can only emerge when accompanied by the knowledge of the environment you are entering.

1

Physical Conditioning and Mental Attitude

Regardless of the type of winter travel you choose, from snow-shoeing to mountaineering, the better shape you are in, the easier and safer it will become and the more you will enjoy it. However, it doesn't have to be a situation in which you beat your body to death. Cross-country skiing, for example, can be as mild as a walk in the park on a summer day; or it can be one of the most grueling outdoor sports known to man. The choice is entirely up to you, but any physical conditioning you do should be based on that choice. One word of caution here: because of the wide range of different skier's abilities and because you will be expected to travel some distance with your companions, try to choose those with similar interests and abilities. A slow recreational skier would quickly become a burden to a group of racing types. Conversely, the racing type might become a pain in the butt to a slower skier who is trying to keep up. But whatever you choose, you should have a fairly good idea of the general conditioning that will make the sport more enjoyable.

Height/Weight Balance

Simple physics tells us that it takes one foot-pound of energy to raise each pound of your weight a distance of one foot. If you are 10 pounds overweight and take a trip requiring an altitude gain of 5,000 feet, 50,000 additional foot-pounds of energy will be required. This is about the amount of energy it takes to lift a Cadillac 10 feet. It doesn't make much sense to carry around any more weight than is needed.

Take a quick look at the optimum height/weight chart for men and women. If you fall into the overweight class it will be to your advantage to lose a few pounds.

1

Optimum Height/Weight for Men and Women

MEN

HEIGHT	SMALL FRAME	MEDIUM FRAME	LARGE FRAME
5'3''	121	131	141
5'4''	124	135	144
5'5''	128	138	148
5'6''	131	141	152
5'7''	134	145	156
5'8''	138	149	160
5'9''	141	152	164
5'10''	145	156	168
5'11''	148	160	172
6'0''	152	165	177
6'1''	156	169	181
6'2''	160	173	186
6'3''	164	178	191
6'4''	168	182	196
6'5''	173	187	201

WOMEN

HEIGHT	SMALL FRAME	MEDIUM FRAME	LARGE FRAME
4'10''	95	103	111
4'11''	98	106	114
5'0''	101	109	117
5'1''	104	112	120
5'2''	106	115	124
5'3''	109	118	127
5'4''	112	122	131
5'5''	116	125	134
5'6''	119	128	138
5'7''	122	132	142
5'8''	126	136	146
5'9''	129	140	150
5'10''	133	143	154
5'11''	136	147	158
6'0''	140	152	163
6'1''	144	156	167
6'2''	148	160	172

Exercise Programs

In any sport there are participants who are secret members of The International Association of Men of Mighty Muscles, Ltd. These people are often fine fellows, but they seem to get their kicks in reaching the apex of muscular perfection and quietly observing their "inferiors." Unless you are a card-carrying member of this association do not try to keep up with them. Trying to keep up can kill a person. You are the best qualified to determine your own limitations and abilities. Stick well within them both while training and in the field.

Any sport is for pleasure, not self-abuse. Therefore, match your exercise program to your intended sport. Overtraining wastes both time and effort. Maintain an even level of physical conditioning, one that is sufficient to allow participation in the sport of your choosing at the level appropriate for your abilities. If you wish to snowshoe in the winter, do a lot of hiking in the summer. Should you wish to enter amateur cross-country ski races, a year-round program of running is certainly in order.

It is important to keep in mind that good conditioning can be measured by your heart rate and blood pressure. You should condition to a level where you are able to function well without your heart pounding or your blood pressure leaping off the scale. That's not to say you have to run around with a blood pressure gauge, but do be aware of your heart rate or the feeling of blood pounding in your throat and temples.

Riding a bike is perhaps the most beneficial exercise and is an excellent alternative method of transportation (nearly pollution free, body odor notwithstanding). Using stairs instead of elevators, parking at the back of parking lots so that you have to walk a little farther and taking brisk walks at lunch time can also help you to get a bit of exercise during your daily routines. When you do walk, walk as though you have someplace to go; breathe deeply and take long strides. Staying active with sports such as tennis or swimming are naturally excellent ways to maintain muscular and respiratory tone. Beyond these, there are some exercises that are very helpful. Many can be found in skiing magazines and other publications in their fall editions. Also, the United States Ski Association publishes an excellent booklet with detailed programs of ski exercises which is available through their regional offices. And many local colleges and adult education programs offer pre-ski conditioning classes.

Here are a few basic toning exercises.

Leg Raises — Hang from an overhead bar with both arms. Just relax, allowing the abdominal muscles, lower back muscles and spine to relax and stretch. Draw your legs up into a horizontal position and then lower them. At first, you can keep your knees bent. Later, for more toughening, keep your legs straight. Breathe deeply with each movement. The exercise is fantastic, slimming the waist and hips, and it builds chest muscles. But, more importantly, it builds abdominal and pelvic muscles while stretching and straightening the spine.

Duck Walking — With your spine upright and straight and your hands on your hips, squat down until you are about halfway between a full squat and standing. Walk this way. It's great for all leg muscles.

Toe Raises—Standing with the balls of your feet on a two-by-four, heels extending off the block, allow the heels to go down to touch the floor. Then stretch up on your toes as high as possible. This strengthens the muscles of the lower leg.

Leg Stretches—Sit on the floor with your legs spread out in front of you and bend forward to touch your forehead to the floor. This will stretch your hamstrings and help to prevent "charlie horses."

Splits—Another good leg stretch exercise is the splits, stretching the legs out to the sides and going as low to the floor as possible. If done while hanging from a bar, this is an extremely valuable, but difficult exercise.

Thigh Stretches—Sit on your heels with legs bent backward under you, lean backward as far as possible at first, supporting yourself with your hands behind you. Later this can be done without support and, with your spine held straight, it can be made into a situp exercise. This exercise is important because if the muscles in the front of the thigh are too tight they will pull the front of the pelvis downward, thus increasing the curve of the lower back. The resulting swayback is fatiguing and painful, especially with a pack on your back.

Add to these a few situps, chinups and pushups and you'll have a routine designed to turn any mild-mannered reporter into a phone-booth stripper. So, a word of advice on when to exercise is in order. Never exercise before bedtime. What you would be doing is pumping your muscles full of lactic acid from your work. If you then lie down you do not give the muscles a chance to excrete the lactic acid and other waste products which cause you to feel stiff and tired. This is the main cause of the pain in the old bod the next morning. Exercise earlier in the day; then your daily activity will allow the muscles to work themselves out and you will have far less trouble with soreness.

This brings up another worthwhile point. After a day of strenuous activity on skis or snowshoes, don't just jump into your car and drive back to the city nonstop. This allows the lactic acid deposits to build up in the muscles. Stop occasionally at a turn out, get out of the car and run, breathe deeply and stretch. This activity will prevent drowsiness and may even prevent an accident. It is not the exercise, but the stiffening up from sitting around afterward that makes people so sore.

A point for women to remember is that wearing high-heeled shoes may give you great-looking calves in the office, but it shortens the Achilles' tendon in the back of your legs. When wearing flat ski boots, the restretching of these muscles and tendons is most unpleasant. Also, if you do spend a couple of days on skis and then go back to the office with the good old high heels, it may be the cause of sore legs. A good exercise to stretch the tendon is to stand barefoot with the ball of the foot on a two-by-four or brick. Raise up on your toes and then drop your heels down to touch the floor. Repeat. This exercise will strengthen the muscles and stretch the tendon.

Mental Attitudes

Physical conditioning is, of course, quite important. But mental conditioning is even more important. Before you start out into the wilds in the winter it's a good idea to get your head together.

When a man sets out to conquer the elements, it is not the elements that are conquered. When you leave the familiar routines of your corner of civilization to travel into the wilderness, you can't approach it as a stranger and struggle to force your will upon nature. When entering into a new environment you must strive to blend with nature and become a part of it. Obey nature's rules. If you have any questions as to what they are, stop and look at what is going on around you.

No animal ventures out in a severe storm; neither should a human. If caught in a storm, find a warm place and wait it out. The same philosophy goes for any other activity in the wild. Look about to see what is going on and don't try to force activities that conditions do not warrant. Take your time, conserve energy, and move slowly enough to see and feel more of the countryside. Again, think of the animals — they never run unless fleeing from danger or chasing their dinner.

It is also a good practice to plan any trip well in advance. The planning and the expectation are often much of the fun. Working out.the details of routes and equipment will allow a trip to move more smoothly and you will be better prepared to cope with any changes which might come up. Rigid, minute-by-minute plans are a burden, but each member of the party should be completely informed as to routes, equipment, the ability of his companions and what is expected of him. Being caught unprepared out in the woods can ruin an otherwise fine trip.

Along with planning the trip, it is important to become acquainted with your companions and to take their feelings into consideration. Treat them with respect and try to see their side of any question. When tired, cold or under stress, tempers and judgment often fail, even among the best of friends. Should you become tired and begin to drag, a faster, stronger skier who keeps pulling out in front can become an object of pure hate. Likewise, the stronger skier may feel impatient and resent the plodding pace of a slower companion. If you find yourself doing a slow burn over such a situation, stop and talk it over.

Many parties have gone along to disaster with no one wanting to be the first to speak up and say that he's too cold, too tired, scared or too hungry. Chances are there are others who feel about the same way and they are just waiting for someone else to speak up. Rather than march along courting some form of disaster, speak up. Then stop and talk it over and figure out how to fix the situation before it gets out of hand.

When you go out in the wilderness leave your pride and ego at home. Compared to the mountains and forests you're a scrawny little critter and all your stomping and racing about only serve to make you look foolish. Be a bit humble and quiet; if you're any good, people will notice you and will have a great deal more respect for you. Being good on skis or good in the woods shows up very clearly. When someone asks for help or advice give it in as friendly a manner as possible without showing off just how smart you are. If you see someone doing something wrong it works best to *suggest,* not tell, them another way to accomplish their purpose.

Now a short commercial for nature. Making a city dump out of a park or wild area is just plain dumb. Do not go about tearing up or cutting down the countryside. There just isn't enough left to go around. Pack out every single scrap of waste material. Burying it under the snow will only hide it until the spring thaw. Broken-down trees and fire-scarred rocks are also not beauty marks in the woods. A slogan commonly used which should be followed like the law goes, "Take only pictures, leave only foot prints." To this I might add, "Keep good memories."

One item which should never be left at home and is more welcome on a trip than anything else is a good sense of humor. To be able to see the humor in a situation and laugh about things when they are not going just right is a very valuable asset. If your snowshoes get tangled in the underbrush and you go sprawling in the soft snow with a pack on your back, and all you do is sit there and laugh instead of ranting and raving, then your head and the rest of your world are probably in a pretty good place.

I suppose this chapter could go on forever. We could discuss the dangers of panic and all of the facets of thinking straight. But what it all adds up to is a few simple rules: Keep calm, stay relaxed and maintain a good sense of humor. Stay alert and keep in touch with what's going on around you. Above all, treat the environment and your companions with respect. With this sort of mental attitude, some preparation and common sense, you can make any outing a memorable and worthwhile experience.

Related Reading

U.S. Ski Association, *Physical Conditioning Hand-book*. USSA, Denver, CO, 1976

The editors of Sports Illustrated, *Sports Illustrated Book of Skiing*. J.B. Lippincott, Philadelphia and New York, 1960

Royal Canadian Air Force, *Exercise Plans for Physical Fitness*. Simon and Schuster, New York, 1962

Painter, Hal, *The Cross Country Ski Cook, Look and Pleasure Book*. Wilderness Press, Berkeley, CA, 1973

Leuchs, Arne and Skalka, Patricia, *Ski with Yoga:Conditioning for the Mind and Body*, Greatlakes Living Press, Matteson, IL, 1976

U.S. Forest Service, USDA and U.S. Ski Association, *Winter Recreation Safety Guide*. USDA, Washington, D.C., USDA Program Aid No. 1140, 1976

2

Weather

There are three main factors of weather that are of concern to the outdoorsman: wind, moisture and temperature. These and a fourth, rather special factor, lightning, and their interaction will govern all your actions while your are in the wilderness. We shall go over each one separately; but remember that when more than one of the factors is present, each greatly increases the effect of the others.

Wind

Wind cools a body by convection. That is, it moves the warm air that is close to your skin away from you. The air that replaces it is cooler, so your body has to work to warm up the new air which is constantly being replaced by still newer cool air. For this reason a windbreaker jacket should be worn over all other clothing to prevent the wind from literally blowing the warm air out of your other clothes. A windbreaker worn under other clothes would make the outer garments nearly useless, due to air loss.

Wind is also a fatiguing factor. Walking into a strong wind requires much more energy than is needed for normal walking. Just holding yourself erect in a strong or gusty wind requires much extra work from the postural muscles and will cause rapid fatiguing.

In addition to its cooling and fatiguing effects on the human body, wind moves things, especially storm clouds and snow. It is, therefore, vital that you check the direction of the prevailing wind (the direction from which the wind, in a given area, tends to blow most of the time).

As a general rule, weather fronts travel across the country

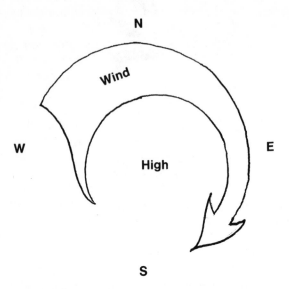

N

W   **E**

S

Fair weather systems are characterized by high barometric pressure and a clockwise flow of air around their centers.

from west to east. In the central states, however, this may not hold true since low pressure centers often travel north from the Gulf. Also, those cold winter storms can drop down along the Rockies from Canada.

Fair weather systems are characterized by high barometric pressure and a clockwise flow of air around their centers, while storm systems are characterized by low barometric pressure and a counter clockwise flow of air. Therefore, if you are in an area where the prevailing wind is from the west and the present flow of air is from the north, this can indicate you are on the lead edge of a high pressure zone. Hence, the next few hours should bring good weather. Likewise, it could indicate you are on the trailing edge of a low pressure zone, which means that a storm system is passing. But remember, the fact that one storm is passing is no guarantee that another storm is not right behind the first one. So, if the wind shifts back to a southerly direction, you may be in for another storm.

If you find yourself on the edge of a weather system which is passing either to the north or south of you, the east-west flow of wind may be the telling direction.

Look at the clouds to see where they are piled up or where the sky is clear. With your compass, determine their location and the direction of the wind and cloud movements. With this information and some quick calculations based on the clockwise/counterclockwise flow of air within weather systems in field weather predictions, you can at least get a bit of a start.

It is also wise to remember that mountains, valleys and other terrain factors can alter ground wind patterns. Do not always judge the flow of winds aloft by the ground winds.

If you fail in your early attempts at weather forecasting, take heart. Remember the batting average of your local weatherman and keep trying. The practice will make you more aware of the environment and its changes. With a few years' experience, you too can squint at the sky, spit into the wind and utter those immortal words, "yup, there's a storm blowing up," with at least a 50-50 chance you will be right.

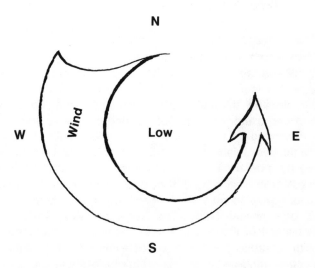

Storm systems are characterized by low barometric pressure and a counterclockwise flow of air.

Wind drift pattern has formed in this wind-packed snow.

Wind also moves snow, causing it to pile up in drifts in shel-
tered places and to sweep the windward sides of hills almost
bare. In the mountains this can be one of the single most important factors in the building of avalanche conditions. As snow
falls during a storm, it may be carried across an exposed slope
and deposited on the lee side of the hill. A mild storm with only
a few inches of snow may build up many feet of snow on the
sheltered side of a hill. It may also cause the formation of a
cornice, or overhanging drift of snow at the top of a ridge. Cornices can grow to massive weights that can later come crashing
down onto anyone below. Therefore, in selecting a route, it may
be warmer traveling along a lee slope, out of the wind, but you
may be courting disaster from an avalanche. It is safer to travel
the colder wind-swept slopes. Think before you go.

Wind will also cause a settling of the snow as the snow shifts
back and forth. This is known as wind pack, and the snow, so

Snow has blown clear of this mountain and lies piled at the base of the cliff.

packed, will more easily support the weight of a traveler. Remember that if you move into the lee of a large rock or other wind break, the snow may not be packed and you may suddenly come to an unexpected stop.

The direction of the prevailing wind is of such importance that it must become a point of constant evaluation whenever you are in the field. Land features alter wind patterns even when the winds aloft may be blowing from a constant direction. Mountains, canyons, ridges and even large trees and boulders affect the wind currents along the ground. Because ground wind is one of the major factors determining the condition of the snow pack, which in turn directly affects your travel, you must check the wind direction carefully.

Observe the patterns in the snow caused by the sculpture of the wind. Small drift lines, complete with miniature cornices, may well be in evidence. Look along high ridges to see if there are snow plumes blowing off the summit or if an overhanging cornice might be present. Large or small, the tip of a cornice always points away from the direction of the prevailing wind. Check about large rocks or the trunks of trees and observe drifting. Trees may be strongly twisted or bent with most of their branches pointing one direction. This is a common indicator of the prevailing wind in a given area. But do not fool yourself—on any given day or during any particular storm, the wind might be blowing from the opposite direction. Just because the wind usually blows from one direction does not mean that it always does, so the snow patterns may be confused.

Temperature

If you are cold, you don't feel well and you don't think or work well. All body functions slow down and the body has to expend energy just to keep itself warm. Get cold enough, long enough, and you will die. This fact alone is enough to make the winter mountaineer become very conscious of temperature changes. In winter, changes of only a few degrees can greatly alter the entire environment.

There are a few physical laws that apply to heat, its conduction and its effect on matter. Keep them in mind. First, there is

Trail of a skier

the effect of heat on the air: hot air rises and cold air settles. On warm sunny days, as the valleys heat up, the air begins to rise and you will notice an uphill flow of air, especially during the afternoon. As the sun goes down this will quickly change. The colder air off the peaks begins to settle, causing a downhill flow. But remember: For this effect to take place, what you might think of as warm air is not required. The only requirement is that the valley air be warmer than the air lying above it. So it is the relative difference in temperature that causes the flow of these ground winds, rather than an actual blast of hot or cold air.

It is this change in the air flow that is often responsible for the time-honored custom of smoke from a campfire suddenly blowing into the cook's face. Perhaps there was one time when you set up camp in the late afternoon when there was still an uphill flow of wind, with the work area upwind from the camp-fire. Then, as dinner time rolled around and you sat around watching the sunset, the wind did its about-face. Suddenly you found yourself downwind from the fire, your eyes and nose smarting from smoke.

When selecting a campsite, remember that the warm, shel-tered little pothole valley may look great in the afternoon, but when night comes and the cold air begins to settle down, it may become the coldest spot around. This is especially true of can-yons, which form natural funnels for cold winds to whip through at night.

Also, open water evaporates. Hence, if you camp near open water, evaporation will increase the moisture content of the air that you'll be sleeping in. Damp air has a far greater cooling ef-fect than does dry air; so, you are colder. In addition, a damp sleeping bag—especially a down bag—is not the warmest place in the world.

Considering these factors, it is often best to build your camp a little higher on a hillside and away from a stream or pond.

Snow conditions are dependent on temperature. Changes of only a few degrees can greatly alter the consistency of the snow. This is certainly known to the cross-country skier who must match his waxes to the snow conditions. As the tempera-ture rises, the surface of the snow becomes wetter, and softer waxes must be used. In the late afternoon and evening, as the temperature drops, the surface may cool or freeze to form a hard or icy crust. This may support the traveler better, but it may also require some different waxes and travel techniques.

The top few inches of the snow pack are very dependent on temperature changes and the crystalline formation of the snow alters vastly with only a degree or two of change. As it is these few upper inches of snow which most affect your means of travel, it becomes important to keep these changes in mind. At night you may be able to wander about on a good firm snow pack without trouble. But by mid-morning of the next day, you might break through the crust and wallow about in snow up to your belt buckle.

This can be a little tricky: In sunny weather the warming and freezing effect may settle the snow in the open. But in the shade, under trees, the sun may not have melted the snow and it will not have settled. The cross-country skier may come sweeping down across a sunny hillside on well-packed, settled snow, but as he enters the woods at the bottom he may hit cold, unsettled powder. The sudden deceleration this causes can produce some of the more interesting experiences known to skiers.

The converse can also happen if the temperature has been generally warm in recent days. All of the snow may have crusted over. But in the sun the crust can melt, while remaining frozen in the shade. Then the skier will move down the open hill on damp, relatively slow snow to hit ice under the trees. This sudden change can yield an impromptu ballet worthy of Walt Disney, but accompanied by un-Disneylike utterances.

Air temperature and the air's general moisture content can be an early indicator of weather changes. Become aware of the feel of the air; a cold damp wind may be the forerunner of a storm.

Sudden rises in temperature may cause a melting and shifting within the snow pack, which could result in avalanches. Heat travels from regions of high temperature to regions of lower temperature. The rate at which any material conducts heat away from its source is important. Of course metals are the best conductors of heat. Therefore, handling cold metal draws heat away from your hands to heat the metal, making your hands very cold, very quickly. Still air is a poor conductor of heat. For example, in a thermos bottle it is the dead (still) air space between the walls of the bottle that maintains the heat within the inner bottle. So it is with your clothing. To a great degree it is the dead air trapped between successive layers of clothes that will keep you warm. When traveling, try to keep yourself in a comfortable state; take off a layer or two while exerting and generating heat, and add an extra layer or two during rest breaks.

Moisture

Moist air behaves somewhat differently than dry air. While air is poor conductor of heat, water is a fairly good one when motionless, which it seldom is. When in motion, water is a very good conductor indeed. Get water on the body and it will literally draw heat out, leaving the body to warm the water. This is why you are cooled by sweating and why, if you get wet while out in the mountains, you are apt to freeze your tail feathers.

The only natural fiber material which can get wet and still maintain its heat-retaining ability is wool. However, several firms are now manufacturing synthetic fibers such as Dacron Fiber Fill II and Polar Guard which have remarkable heat-retaining qualities when wet. So in damp climates these should also be carefully considered. A down jacket may be super warm, but if it gets wet it's about as good as a wet T-shirt.

In nature, moisture comes as fog, clouds, rain, freezing rain, hail and snow. Fog is a cloud within 50 feet of the ground. It is usually the result of condensation in the air near the earth. In the mountains, however, it may be the result of clouds drifting onto the slopes or passing across the tops of the peaks. It can be raining or snowing or both at once (which is pure joy) in fog.

Fog usually consists of water droplets, but may also consist of ice crystals. This latter circumstance is especially true in the case of clouds drifting onto the mountains. In such circumstances clothes may become iced up as stiff as a board in minutes. As a general rule, fog seldom produces precipitation in large amounts at lower elevations. However, this is not the case in the mountains.

Visibility is limited in fog, so your traveling may have to be slowed down or even halted until your direction can be established. An occurrence in snow country which can be most disturbing is known as a "white out." It can occur on either cloudy or sunny days. What happens is that when a cloud moves in, the light filtering through the fog reflects off the snow and turns the fog as white as the snow. Under these conditions you are unable to tell where the snow and sky meet. All sense of distance, direction and size are distorted. A tin can placed at one's feet may appear to be a 55-gallon oil drum, many yards distant. The edge of a cliff may appear to be a smooth field. If caught in a white out, be very cautious and travel by compass or not at all. Do not let companions out of your sight—which may mean only a few feet away.

A fundamental knowledge of types of clouds and the likelihood of their producing rain or snow is most important. There are 10 main cloud genera (families) which are subdivided into fourteen species, based on shape, and nine varieties, based on transparency. To go into a detailed study would not serve our purposes. But to recognize general cloud types and the probability of precipitation with each is useful. The main division of clouds, based on altitude (cloud altitude is measured from ground level, not sea level), is:

High (16,500 to 45,000 feet)
 Cirrus—Detached clouds in the form of white delicate filaments (hairlike)
 Cirrocumulus—White cloud patch composed of small elements in the form of ripples
 Cirrostratus—Transparent, whitish cloud veil of fibrous or smooth appearance, totally or partly covering the sky
Middle (16,500 to 23,000 feet)
 Altocumulus—White or gray patch, sheet or layer of cloud with shadowing, composed of laminae, rounded masses, rolls
 Altostratus—Grayish or bluish cloud sheet or layer striated, fibrous or uniform in appearance, totally or partly covering sky and having thin places to reveal the sun
 Nimbostratus—Gray cloud layer, often dark, blots out sun, appears diffused by continuously falling rain or snow. Low ragged clouds often occur below the layer.
Low (0 to 6,500 feet)
 Stratocumulus—Gray or whitish patch sheet or layer of cloud with dark spots composed of checkerboard patterns, rounded masses, rolls
 Stratus—Gray cloud layer with a fairly uniform base, may give drizzle, ice prisms or snow. Sun may be visible.
 Cumulus—Detached clouds generally dense with sharp outlines. Develop vertically in the form of rising mounds, domes or towers, with the bulging upper parts resembling cauliflower. The sunlit parts are brilliant white; the base quite dark.

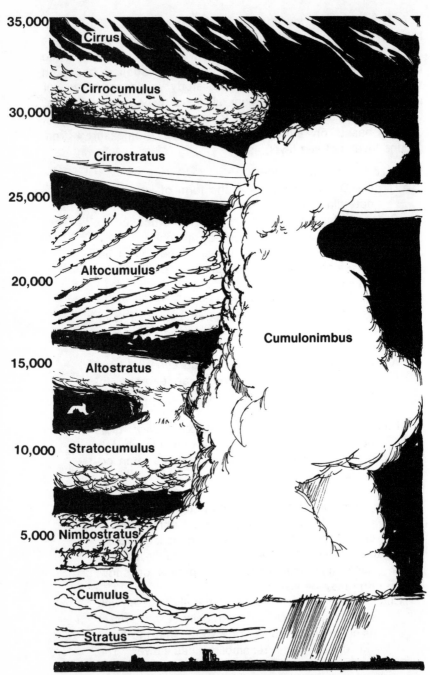

Knowing cloud types and the likelihood of their producing rain or snow is essential for the outdoorsperson.

Cumulonimbus—Heavy dense cloud, considerable
vertical extent (mountain or huge tower). The
top is smooth and often flattened in the shape
of an anvil or vast plume. Low, ragged clouds
often appear at the bottom of the cloud.

Precipitation in significant amounts usually only falls from altostratus, nimbostratus and cumulonimbus clouds. Precipitation
may fall from altocumulus, stratocumulus, stratus or cumulus,
but amounts are usually small. Stratus clouds may produce a
drizzle, whereas cumulus clouds are usually accompanied by
heavy showers or thunderstorms. Steady rain is produced from
altostratus or nimbostratus clouds.

For the back country traveler, and especially for the mountaineer, it is most important to be able to analyze the prevailing
conditions and determine the possibility of a change in the
weather. It is not necessary to become a meteorologist. However, being aware of the clouds and their meaning, as well as
watching for wind and temperature changes, will give you a fair
warning of possible trouble. There are areas of the country, particularly in northern New England and the northern plains states,
where the weather can change in a matter of minutes. But in the
western U.S., changes are usually evident at least an hour or so
beforehand.

It doesn't take a weather prophet to see storm clouds building
on the horizon or closing in around the top of your mountain. It
does take someone with common sense to turn back before it is
too late and trouble descends. In such cases the 180-degree
turn is the greatest safety precaution known to man.

Somewhat less obvious are the more subtle changes in the
environment: a slight rise or fall in the temperature, a gust of
wind from a new direction, a sudden feeling of dampness in the
air, an unusual quiet or birds which no longer chirp, but sit quietly in the trees. Sometimes, even on a very personal level,
there can be a feeling within yourself that something is wrong.
These should not be taken at once as signs of danger. But they
should be examined in the light of other weather indicators and
the degree of commitment you are making on your trip. How far
are you planning to go, and how long will it take you to return in
bad weather should you decide you have to turn back?

Here are a few well-established weather indicators that should
be kept in mind.

If you observe high "horsetails" of cirrus or cirrostratus clouds moving in, and they appear to be thickening and lowering to altostratus, a storm is imminent. In the Sierra this is a frequent occurence in the late afternoon.

A ridge of clouds appearing on the horizon, especially if they are in the direction of the flow of the weather system, is a certain warning of storms.

A halo or ring around the sun or moon is an indication of high ice crystals that are often the forerunners of storm systems.

In the spring, thunderstorms most frequently occur on the leading edge of a cold air mass. If you hear or see a spring thunderstorm you may expect a drop in the temperature to occur.

In the evening a low dense overcast acts like a blanket and prevents rapid cooling of the air. A clear sky usually accompanies a much colder night.

A layer of stratocumulus clouds and a strong wind in the morning will indicate a cold cloudy day with little or no temperature rise to be expected.

Lightning

As a general rule, lightning is not a great problem for the winter traveler. It is included, however, because in many areas of the country, cross-country skiing and ski mountaineering can be enjoyed well into the spring months, when the danger from electric storms is greatly increased. Lightning is a frequent outdoor killer.

Simply speaking, lightning is a spark that jumps between regions of excessive electrical charge. There are three types of lightning:

Cloud to earth —The *down stroke* is the most frequent form of lightning. It usually strikes the highest object around in a flat area. While a down stroke can strike someone, it usually causes a breakdown of voltage in the air around the body and the victim sustains only a few thousand volts of so-called arc voltage for a fraction of a microsecond. This can kill, but in the majority of cases, people recover completely.

Earth to cloud — The *upstroke lightning* is by far the most lethal. It usually strikes only high promontories. A victim may be exposed for several hundredths of a second to as many as 100 to 300 amperes and to temperatures as high as 50,000°F. This is almost always fatal. Body and clothes are burned and metal objects are melted or welded together.

When lightning strikes, its charge is dissipated in an expanding circle around the point of impact. It is the conduction of current produced by this voltage gradient that is responsible for most casualties. Of course, the nearer you are to the strike, the worse things are.

As the current spreads out, it follows the path of least resistance or the best conductor. It follows cracks, small streams, lines of vegetation; it will run down the face of a cliff, or jump through small caves. In seeking shelter, avoid such areas. Spread your group out at least 10 to 12 yards apart. If caught in the open, ditch all metal objects and crouch low on the best insulation available (insolite pad, rope coil, etc.) but do not lie down.

The greatest danger in any electrical shock comes when the current flows through a vital organ. If the current flows from one hand to the other through the arm and across the chest it will pass through the heart and lungs. A current passing through the head to the feet will involve nearly every organ in the body, especially the brain and spinal cord. On the other hand, the body can stand a considerable amount of current passing from one leg to the other; so you should crouch rather than lie or sit on the ground. Add to this any insulating effect from boots, insolite pad, rope coil, etc. and you can be reasonably safe from all but the most direct strike.

In a tent, remember that the tent poles stick up. It may be dry, but it's not too safe a place. Above all, if you should ever notice your metal gear start to buzz, the head of an ice ax start to glow (St. Elmo's Fire), a tingling or electrical feeling in the legs and the feeling that your hair is standing up, drop everything and get out fast!

Electrical storms are so frequent that if you spend much time outdoors, you will certainly have to deal with lightning in one way or another. Lightning often strikes not only twice but many times in the same place because it is drawn to the highest and best conductor around.

In addition, remember that thunderstorms travel at speeds in excess of 25 mph. Don't try to outrun them; wait the storm out in a safe place:

Between large flat rocks
Crouching low on insulation
50 to 80 feet from the face of a cliff
In the center of a spacious dry cave
Among a stand of small trees
Off exposed ridges

Conclusion

If you are to be out in the wilds, especially in the winter, it is important to keep track of the weather reports in your favorite haunts. A running account or log of weather conditions in the mountains may be a most useful tool for knowing what snow conditions may be expected. Early warmer snows may settle into a firm base and adhere well to mountain sides. A cold spell prior to the early storms can freeze the ground before the snow falls and may mean a loose layer of snow with poor adhesion. A period of very warm weather may cause a melting of the surface of the snow pack, which could be followed by a cold snap producing a layer of ice. If this is then overlaid by a cold dry snowfall, there will be poor adhesion between the layers, leading to avalanche danger.

Knowing the amount of snow that usually falls during an average winter storm in a given area is also quite valuable. If most storms tend to add only a few inches, that is one thing; but if several feet of snow can accumulate in a single storm, that's quite another problem. In the Pacific Northwest, storms commonly dump large amounts of snow in a short period of time.

Knowing whether any storm was accompanied or followed by periods of high winds will also foretell the location of the snow once it has reached the ground. With the wind, you should expect drifts and deep snow on the slopes.

These factors will be discussed in a later section on avalanches. For the moment, remember that if you know what's been happening in the mountains and can adapt yourself and your equipment to the environment, you will be a much happier and safer back country traveler. *Weather is the killer of the unprepared.* Forget your rain gear, windbreaker or extra jacket or mess up on your shelter and you may not have to regret it for very long.

The small trees being bent by snow creeping downhill is an avalanche danger sign.

Related Reading

Lehr, P.E., R.W. Burnett, and H.S. Zim, *Weather.* Golden Press, New York, 1957

Day, J.A. and G.L. Sternes, *Climate and Weather.* Addison-Wesley, Menlo Park, CA , 1970

Miller, A., and J. C. Thompson, *Elements of Meteorology.* Charles E, Merrill Co., Columbus, OH, 1975

LaChapelle, E.R., *Field Guide to Snow Crystals.* University of Washington Press, Seattle, WA, 1969

U.S. Dept. of Commerce, N.O.A.A. *Explanatory Sheet for Daily Weather Maps.* Superintendent of Documents, Government Printing Office, Washington, D.C.

3

Avalanche Safety

An avalanche is a mass of snow on a slope that begins to move rapidly downhill when its frictional resistance is overcome. In this section we will discuss why snow builds up on a slope, the terrain on which this happens and the mechanisms that can cause the snow to break loose and start an avalanche. We will also discuss methods of travel on and around avalanche zones and the rescue techniques used when there is an accident. By far the single most important lesson to be learned regarding avalanches is how to recognize their zones and how to avoid getting caught in one. Once again, *prevention is the name of the game.*

Where

Avalanche zones occur on snow-covered slopes with an angle of between 15 and 65 degrees. Smaller avalanches, or sluffs, occur in a range up to 80 degrees. The most dangerous avalanches originate on slopes that have an angle of from 30 to 45 degrees. The slope may be either convex or concave. Convex slopes are more apt to yield a slab avalanche than concave slopes. However, both are quite capable of sliding. Most avalanches occur in slide zones where they have occurred before. The zone may be a short hill, only a hundred yards long, or it may encompass an entire mountainside, extending for miles. The most dangerous areas are on open slopes and in steep gullies. Anything that impairs the movement of the snow downhill serves to reduce the danger. Heavily wooded slopes, ridges, terraces, large boulders or outcroppings form natural barriers. Avalanche zones are often difficult to recognize, so a good understanding of the terrain and close observation are vital.

Summer Travel. Summer travel is an important part of the understanding of winter hazards. In summer, when the snow cover is gone, the terrain features are more evident and the ground cover is exposed. Look for areas where avalanches have occurred. There will be a slope wiped clean of large vegetation, with stands of trees on both sides of a swath running up and downhill. In the Rockies such a zone may have been filled with fast-growing aspen, while the remainder of the hill is covered with firs. A band of aspen extending up and down a hill is a good indication that at some time a slide has occurred. Sometimes a pile of debris, broken tree limbs and rocks may mark the terminal point of a slide. In some areas, the tops of smaller trees are ripped off, while the lower portions of the trees, which were protected by deeper snow, may remain intact. The uphill sides of trees may show scars where the bark was torn off by a previous avalanche.

Look at the ground cover for its ability to hold snow. Smooth unbroken slopes will not hold snow as well as those strewn with boulders or heavily covered with vegetation. When traveling during the summer, try to think of the average depth of snow that the area receives in the winter. If the slope is covered with six-foot-high manzanita or slash brush, then it could be expected to hold about the same depth of snow before it would be likely to slide. Trees make a good natural barrier against avalanches. The more heavily wooded the slope, the less likely it is to slide.

However, remember that avalanches may start higher up on the slope above the tree line, and build up sufficient energy to plow through even the most densely wooded area. A long, grass-covered hill will offer no resistance to slides. With the first snow the grass lies flat and forms a natural slide for the snow to glide upon. Glacier-polished granite offers no bond for the snow pack and only a few inches may slide down a slope and leave no tell-tale signs in the summer. Ridges that run up and down a hill will form a natural boundary for an avalanche path, while those running across the fall line of the hill will constitute a dam for the moving snow. Large outcroppings of rock form an island of safety in a slide zone. Benches and terraces may act to hold back a slide, but they may also fill with snow and add tons of weight to the snow pack. Such might be the case with a road or a trail traversing the face of a steep hill.

Winter Travel. With the knowledge of the terrain gathered from summer travel and the location of any old slide zones in mind,

Overhangs of ice along the tops of ridges can fracture without the least warning.

winter travel is much safer. If you have been unable to travel in the region during the summer, a careful check with a local ranger, game warden or resident may give you some idea of the location of possible dangerous areas. While you are at it, a check on snow conditions is also in order. Determine the direction of the prevailing wind, because the location of the lee and windward slopes is vital. The windward side of a hill may be swept nearly free of snow or at least covered with hard, wind-packed snow. All of the snow that has blown off the windward side will be deposited on the lee slope.

A lee slope may be loaded with many more times the amount of snow than the surrounding average snow depth would indicate. So a hillside covered with six-foot-high brush may not mean much on a lee slope, even if the average depth of snow in the area is only four feet.

Keep a careful eye out along the ridge lines to determine if there are snow plumes. These indicate that wind blowing across

the top of the ridge may be loading up the tops of gullies, setting them up for future slides. Check also for the possibility of
cornices; do not travel onto them or under them. These sometimes massive overhangs of ice seen along the tops of ridges
can fracture without the least warning. Mentioned later in this
section are a number of warning signs in the snow. Learn these
well and be observant of them whenever you are in the field.

Snow Cover. To understand the various types of avalanches
and their trigger mechanisms it is advisable to have some knowledge of the characteristics of snow and the changes that occur
within the snow pack.

Snow is water vapor that has frozen into various crystalline
forms. The density of the new fallen snow is greatly dependent
on its crystalline shape and, hence, on the air temperature. The
colder the air the lighter the snow density; the nearer the freezing point the higher the density. As each successive winter
storm lays down a layer, the snow pack is built up in strata,
each strata showing the characteristic crystalline structure of its
storm. The wall of a snow pit dug vertically into the snow pack
is an excellent visual display of the weather history of the area.
Layers of soft snow, hard pack crust, ice and moist snow are
found as they were laid down.

As time passes and the snow settles, changes occur with the
structure of the crystals of snow. This change is referred to as
metamorphism. It tends to round off the crystals and convert
them into more rounded grains of ice. This process will obliter-
ate the clear layers of the snow and make it more homogene-
ous.

Other forms of metamorphism—caused by the transfer of
water vapor within the snow pack—may also occur. The refreezing and subsequent formation of new crystals produces a
structure composed of a layer of cup-shaped ice crystals. This
layer is very fragile and may collapse, becoming soft and wet.
This is known as depth hoar and it creates an unstable pack.
This is especially important because the conditions that favor its
formation are prevalent in early winter, thereby affecting the lower layers of the snow pack.

A snow pack acts as if it were a very thick syrup; any snow
lying on a hillside tends to deform and creep downhill. It also
slowly glides over the ground. Both the creep and glide are
greatly affected by temperature. Like a syrup, the snow pack
flows more freely in warmer weather and becomes hard and brit-

The most dangerous avalanches can originate on slopes with an angle of from 30 to 45 degrees.

tle upon freezing. The stresses produced within the pack by uneven creep and glide can be enormous and contribute greatly to the cause of avalanches. Cold snow in the shade of a rock may remain brittle while adjacent snow warmed by the sun may be lubricated. A shearing effect is developed and may overcome the cohesion of the snow, causing it to break loose and fall.

As avalanches are greatly dependent on the actions of melting and refreezing within the snow, it is important to realize when and how this might be taking place.

First, snow is an excellent insulator in that it has a great deal of air trapped within it and dead air spaces make good insulation. Therefore, snow has very low heat conductivity. For this reason snow caves and igloos are warm, beyond the point of just keeping out the wind. This insulating quality also protects the earth from extremes of cold, and prevents many plants from being frozen due to prolonged exposure of their roots to freezing temperatures. It also limits the amount of heat that radiates up into the snow pack from the ground, preventing surface heat from radiating into the snow. Hence the snow at the earth level is almost always 32°, at least in the Temperate Zone.

For a single gram of ice at 32°F to melt, it must absorb 80 calories of heat. No change in temperature occurs. The reverse reaction also occurs; therefore, a great deal of heat exchange must go on at the surface of the snow to cause either freezing or melting.

The greatest single mechanism for heat gain or loss from the snow surface is the movement of the air across the surface of the snow. This process is known as eddy conduction and will only occur when there is motion in the air. Therefore, a warm wind will melt snow far better than any other natural mechanism.

Rain water penetrates the snow exceptionally well, a point to remember in an ice cave. If the rain is warm it carries the heat into the pack and uniformly warms the pack.

Under normal winter circumstances the snow pack gains heat in the day and loses it at night, thus becoming soft and more unstable in the afternoon while freezing at night. Should a warm, damp wind such as a chinook start to blow and a layer of warm clouds appear, the pack may be absorbing vast amounts of heat even at night. All factors work together to produce the overall thermal balance in the snow. Be observant and try to figure out what is happening both at the surface and within the pack. Should the snow absorb enough heat to start the granules of ice melting, each becomes covered with a film of water, lubricating it and producing millions of small ball bearings for the pack to move upon.

Snow also acts as though it were black with regard to infra-red light. In fact, at the heat-producing infrared end of the light spectrum, snow is one of the most nearly perfect black substances in nature. Infrared light is absorbed very readily from the sun's rays, warming the snow pack and causing it to melt during the day. This may occur when the actual air temperature is relatively low. On a clear night, the snow pack then radiates the infrared heat waves into space, causing a loss of heat and freezing of the snow. As a result, even though air temperature actually may not have changed, snow which softened during the day may become hard and firm at night.

As for ultraviolet light, which is the portion of the sun's rays responsible for sunburns, the snow remains white, reflecting nearly 100 percent of these rays.

A loose-snow avalanche begins at a single point with any small mechanical disturbance, moves downhill in a formless mass (expanding as it descends) until it reaches an area that is flat enough to hold the weight of the snow.

Types of Avalanches

There are two basic types of avalanches, loose-snow and slab. Both derive their names from their point of origin. Both may be composed of one or several layers and may contain several varieties of snow. And both may vary greatly in size and shape. The snow condition is the determining factor.

Loose-Snow Avalanches. As snow falls on a slope and builds up it has poor cohesion. On very steep slopes it tends to sluff off readily without appreciable buildup. When the angle is less than 65° considerable buildup is possible and the snow hangs on the slope in a very unstable state. This is especially true in steep gullies or shoots. A loose-snow avalanche begins at a single point with any small mechanical disturbance. Snow falling from a tree or ledge, an icicle breaking and dropping into the snow, a falling rock or any similar action may start the snow

moving downhill, building momentum as it goes. It moves downhill in a formless mass, expanding as it descends, until it reaches an area that is flat enough to hold the weight of the snow.
Loose-snow avalanches containing wet snow are very dangerous
because the weight of the wet snow imparts a great deal of energy and makes them very destructive. In addition, the wet snow
packs solid as soon as it stops moving, freezing into a solid
mass. This is common in Maritime mountain ranges such as the
Sierras.

Slab Avalanches. Slab avalanches originate in older, more settled snow in which there is some cohesion. Instead of a single
point of origin, they begin along a fracture line running across
the hill. There may be a single layer of snow or many layers extending down to the bare ground. The snow may be wet or dry,
hard or soft, but it always will have the characteristic fracture
line. Slab avalanches pose the greatest danger to the winter
traveler, primarily because they can be caused by the victim's
movement across the zone. Often the cutting action of skis moving across the fracture zone and the added weight of the skier
are sufficient to trigger a slide.

The slab avalanche occurs when the snow in a given layer
has sufficient internal cohesion to cause it to act as a single
block, and its attachment to the mountain is sufficiently unstable
to allow it to break free and slide downhill. Hence when the pull
of gravity on the mass of the slab exceeds the strength of its attachment to the mountain or underlying layers, an avalanche will
be produced.

The movement of snow in a slab avalanche differs from that
in a loose-snow avalanche. In the loose-snow avalanche, a small
amount of snow starts moving. It hits more snow and pushes
that down the hill, expanding as it goes. In the slab avalanche, a
large sheet of snow extending across a hill breaks out and
slides down as a single unit. This will likely break up into blocks
which roll and tumble over one another, but the snow from the
lower end of the origional slab will end up on the bottom of the
pile when the avalanche stops. Snow from further up the hill will
pile upon it in successive layers. If you must search for victims
in such areas, try to determine where they were on the slab
when it broke loose.

When

When is an avalanche most likely to occur? The safest answer

The slab avalanche occurs when the snow in a given layer has sufficient internal cohesion to cause it to act as a block, and its attachment to the mountain is stable enough to allow it to break free and slide downhill.

is anytime, especially when you least expect it to happen. In an avalanche zone you should consider the slide ready to go at any minute and take every precaution.

But there are certain danger periods of which you should be aware. In the case of loose-snow avalanches, it is unwise to travel during a heavy snowstorm or for about a day afterward.* A heavy snow followed by a clear, sunny day will set avalanches rumbling off nearly every steep slope. On lee slopes the same precautions should be exercised during or following a high wind. This is often indicated by the presence of a snow plume blowing off the high peaks or ridges. Trees unloading snow after a heavy storm may trigger a loose snowslide. Be especially cautious of sparsely timbered, open slopes on such days.

Slab avalanches are much harder to predict. If you have

*Snow falling at the rate of one inch per hour or faster causes extreme danger. Travel for at least 24 hours thereafter is very hazardous.

doubts, a route change is in order. It is also important to consider a slope dangerous even if it did not move when the first skier crossed. Slabs have been known to break and catch the twenty-seventh man in a column crossing a zone. Almost any shock or vibration to the pack may cause the avalanche to trigger. Even loud noises have created enough of a shock wave to send the snow crashing down the slopes. The weight and movements of a skier and the cutting action of his skis to the upper layer of snow are frequent causes.

There are two critical fracture zones for slab avalanches. One is located at the top of the slab where the snow clings to the remainder of the pack, above the potential slide. The second is at the base of the slab. Often many tons of snow can be supported by a fragile crust of snow. Cut this, and the whole slab descends on your head!

Internal stresses can also build up within the pack and be triggered by sudden temperature change. As a rule, snow freezes at night and thaws during the day. Hence, by mid-afternoon the snow pack may be in a very dangerous state. The lubricating effect of a warm rain is especially dangerous. A sudden spring rain is a common occurrence. So if you are caught on an exposed area by such a rain, move to a safe location at once.

Here are a few danger signs that you should also be aware of and be able to recognize while traveling. They are indications that you are on unstable snow; and if the angle of the hill makes it susceptible to avalanche, you could be in grave danger.

Cracks running across the slope—a very dangerous sign indicating the snows creep downhill. The cracks may be the start of a fracture line. They are produced by the same action which produces a crevasse in a glacier. Cross above such cracks and stay well to the top of the ridge.

Cracks which appear in the snow and seem to run ahead of the skier—a good indicator of unstable snow. Some cracking can be expected right around the skis, but should these cracks start to travel, it is dangerous.

A bow wake moving ahead of the skis—another indication of instability. Again, it's normal for

some bow wake to appear just in front of the
ski tip. However, if you notice the shock wave
out a few feet from the ski, it's bad news.
A hollow, drum-like sound as you pass over
snow—an early indication of an unstable layer
of snow within the pack.
The snow giving suddenly or dropping as you
cross.
The presence of sun balls, snowballs that have
rolled down a hill picking up snow as they go.
Above all, seeing or hearing avalanches on adjacent slopes.

If you have any doubts as to the stability of the snow conditions in a given area it's a good idea to test ski a small slope to
determine it's reactions. Locate a short slope which, if it should
slide, would not carry you into rocks, over a cliff or into any other danger. Adopting all of the safety precautions listed in the following section, "Travel in Avalanche Terrain," test the slope by
skiing across its top. Test skiing is not a beginner's job. Do so
only if you are a qualified skier, and then only if it's absolutely

Anything that impairs the movement of snow downhill, such as
this boulder-strewn slope, will help to reduce the danger of ava-
lanches.

necessary. Avalanches that have run a distance of only 30 feet have been known to kill someone trapped in them. Keep this in mind and do not be eager to show off the test ski operation.

Travel in Avalanche Terrain

There are a number of basic safety precautions for winter travel around and near avalanche zones; the simplest approach is to list them. As you read, try to visualize the conditions that could lead to an avalanche and how each of these rules would be of value.

Never travel alone. This is the cardinal rule of all back country travel any time of year and under any conditions.

Stay off avalanche paths and especially avoid fracture zones.

Conduct the line of march so that only one person at a time will be exposed to danger. The remaining members of the party should keep their eyes glued on that person.

If you must cross an avalanche zone, move quickly, do not take rest stops and certainly do not set up camp.

When crossing a zone, do not go straight across, cut the slope at a downhill angle. This will speed up the crossing, and a fracture is less likely to break loose.

Cross the suspected zone at its top.

Put on a jacket and pull the hood up. Wear gloves and close all openings in your clothes. If you should be trapped your chances of survival are better if snow does not get inside your clothes.

Wear an avalanche cord! This is a 60-foot line of brightly colored cord that is attached firmly around the skier's waist and allowed to trail behind. If caught in a slide, the cord will probably boil up to the surface and give rescuers a means to locate the trapped victim.

Loosen all equipment. take the pole straps off your wrists, release pack straps, possibly carry the pack on one shoulder. Set ski bindings as loose as possible.

Do not consider a slope safe just because it did not

Large boulders help form barriers against avalanches.

slide with the first person across. Maintain a careful watch until the last person is across.

Use islands of safety, such as a large rock outcropping, as much as possible in crossing a zone.

Observe the probable path that a slide might take if it should break loose. Determine whether it might go over a cliff or up against rocks or some other problem. If so, retreat is better than risk.

If a slide starts, yell like mad, drop everything and swim like hell for the surface. Avalanches have a rolling action, so fight to stay on top and not get dragged down. If this fails cover your face and mouth. Try to create as much of an air chamber as possible.

If trapped, stay calm, do not panic. Useless struggle wastes air. If you can dig yourself out, do
so. If not, stay still. Trying to call for help is
useless; sound does not carry well out of
snow.

Before any of the above have to be used, common sense and
prevention are the best precautions. Check with local ranger and
ski patrol stations to ask about snow, avalanche and weather
conditions. Just because you have traveled the area in the summer, do not assume that the same routes are safe for winter
travel. Give them your route plans and an expected time of return. Then when you do return check back in, otherwise you
may have search parties out unnecessarily. Do not allow your
ego or just plain laziness to put you onto an avalanche zone
when a route change is clearly indicated.

Travel in Valleys

The dangers of being caught in an avalanche are greatly reduced, but not entirely eliminated, by traveling along the floor of
a valley. While you are most unlikely to trigger a slide while traveling on flat terrain, one may come rumbling off a mountain and
bury you.

To know just where to travel in the valley is important and
here awareness of snow conditions and observation of the high
ridges seems the only real answer. Obvious signs of danger include snow plumes blowing off a ridge, the presence of large
cornices, sun balls rolling off a slope, small slides breaking
loose, a warming trend following a heavy snowstorm or the fact
that a heavy snow is or just has been falling.

In a flat, wide valley the obvious answer is to stay in the middle, well away from the base of either slope. In a narrower valley it will be necessary to determine which slope presents the
greatest danger. This is where it is useful to know which is the
lee slope once you have determined the more dangerous slope
try to anticipate how far out from the base of the slope an avalanche might travel. Always travel close to the opposite side of
the valley beyond the anticipated base of the slide. In V-shaped
valleys that would fill with snow, the best route is part way up
the opposite slope.

Rescue Procedures

Rescue procedures, like other aspects of winter travel, are easi-

A cornice is an overhanging mass of snow, ice or both, which extends out over the edge of a steep drop. It is formed by the wind blowing snow across a ridge.

ly codified. There aren't many rules here, but all are important.

    A rescue leader must assume command at once and the search should be conducted in a calm, organized manner.

    DO NOT PANIC—Check for further slide danger. Set a watch to warn of further avalanches. Pick a safe escape route in case of further sliding.

    Mark the Last Seen Point—That is the point in the slide path where the victim was last seen. This greatly reduces the area to be searched.

    Quick Search—A fast check of the slide for clues, such as bits of clothing, equipment or an avalanche cord. Mark the location of all clues. Concentrate in the area below the last seen point.

Send for Help—If you are within easy range of
help, send for a larger rescue party. If many
hours would elapse before help could arrive,
start the search with those present. If you are
the sole survivor, then a careful search of the
area must be made before you go for help.
Witnesses should remain at the site to help
guide the search party.

Coarse Probe—Use inverted ski poles, long sticks,
ends of skis or any other pole available. Con-
centrate on the most likely areas of burial,
starting from the bottom and working up.
Check the natural flow line downhill from the
last seen point. Especially look near obstruc-
tions such as boulders, trees or changes in the
slope where a body might become hung up
and, of course, in the debris at the base of the
slide.

Coarse Probe Technique. Searchers form a line across the
slide, facing uphill, each holding his probe in front of himself.
Probers should stand about 10 inches apart with feet spread
about 20 inches. On command, each prober rams his probe into
the snow straight down in front of him. On command, he then
withdraws the probe and advances on short step (24 inches)
and the procedure is repeated. Commands: probes down;
probes up; advance. The probe zone must be marked carefully.
A body under the snow gives a dull resistance to the probe.

The advantage of the coarse probe is speed. This is most important as the likelihood of survival is greatly diminished with the
passage of time. After one hour the chances of finding a victim
alive are only about 30 percent. Because a coarse probe is fast,
if the first sweep fails, it should be repeated—with a slight off-
set of course.

Fine Probe Technique. The techniques used in forming the
probe line giving the commands and marking the perimeters are
the same as those used when conducting a coarse probe. The
difference lies in the spacing of the probes. The probers are or-
dered to probe just in front of their left feet, then straight in
front of themselves, then in front of the right feet. The line then
advances only 12 inches and the probes are repeated.

Fine probe is very slow and is normally introduced as a last
effort by a larger search party. A number of coarse probes

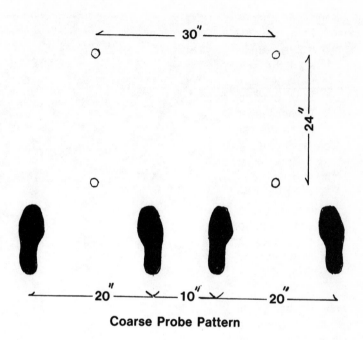

Coarse Probe Pattern

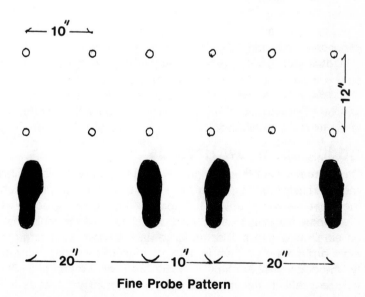

Fine Probe Pattern

Cornices usually appear across the tops of Alpine ridges or high cliffs. They can, however, occur anywhere snow has drifted.

should be tried prior to a fine probe.

A final step used in practice only to recover bodies is the digging of trenches. These are dug vertically up the slide base.

A final note: If a dog is available, avalanche-trained or not, he can be of great help. Even an untrained dog will often dig in the snow where a victim is trapped.

Additional Snow Hazards

Cannonballs. Another danger in cross-country travel is falling rocks. This occurs often as the sun melts snow and ice high on the ridges—particularly in the spring—and loosens rocks, which then come bounding down the slope. These cannonballs may be as small as a golf ball or as large as a trash can or larger. The sight and sound of them is nothing short of terrifying. Fortunately, the odds of being hit are small, but it only takes one. Slopes may be safe in the morning, but be especially cautious in late winter and on spring afternoons. If you should see a rock coming at you, lie flat with your head pointed downhill to give it the smallest target possible. Dodging the damn things is next to impossible. An open area at the base of a steep hill with rocks resting on top of the snow is a tell-tale sign of this danger.

Ice Falls. Another danger in the late winter and spring is an ice fall. As the sun strikes the tops of cliffs it can melt the snow, which then runs down to the face of the cliff. In the shade it can then freeze and form large masses of ice. As more water melts and seeps down around the attachment ot these icicles or ice cornices, they can break loose. Often the spring stillness can be shattered by a booming sound as the ice strikes a ledge part way down the cliff and shatters flying out like so much shrapnel. This is reason enough to keep away from the base of any cliff.

Ice falls are also found in glacier areas where there are multiple crevasses and the system is collapsing. The area is marked by huge blocks of ice larger than a house, and by ice cliffs and crevasses. This is a region only for the experienced mountaineer.

It takes very little to break cornices—they often fall from their weight. Cornices are also frequent causes of avalanches.

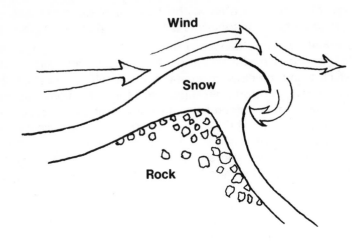

Wind action in building of a cornice.

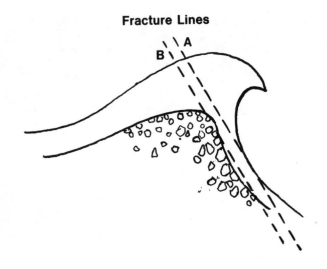

Danger zone on a cornice. Two fracture lines are possible—as the result of just the cornice breaking (fracture line A) or if an avalanche is also triggered (fracture line B). In either case the fracture is never a vertical line through the cornice.

Cornices. A cornice is an overhanging mass of snow, ice or both which extends out over the edge of a steep drop. They are formed by the wind blowing snow across a ridge. On the lee side of the ridge a drift may develop which extends outward over the edge of the ridge. An eddy current in the wind develops behind the protective ridge, causing the base of the overhanging drift to be carved out. This results in the typical cornice structure.

Cornices usually appear across the tops of Alpine ridges or high cliffs. They can, however, occur anywhere snow has drifted. They can just as easily be found along the rim of a gulch, and even small ones can be quite dangerous. Their danger comes from the fact that they are very fragile, often capable of supporting only their own weight. When a traveler steps onto the cornice he may break through. Or the cornice can fracture and send the victim tumbling down the cliff with the cornice on top of him.

Traveling beneath a cornice is almost as dangerous as traveling on top of it. It takes very little to break them and they often fall from their own weight. They are also frequent causes of ava-

A fast-running brook or creek will carve out a considerable stream tunnel, often extending beyond the stream and containing a cave-like air chamber above the stream.

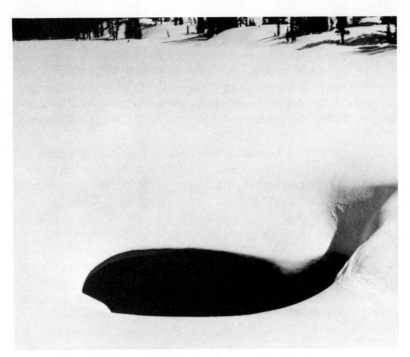

If you are traveling in an area where you know a stream to be running or where you suspect one to be, observe the contour of the snow. Frequently, there will be a linear depression running over the streambed where the snow has sagged.

lanches. When a cornice does fracture it does not break on a simple vertical line. It will, instead, follow a line parallel to the actual slope of its attachment to the mountain. As a result, you should not only keep off cornices but also stand well back toward the windward side of the structures.

Stream Tunnels. Similar to cornices in their formation are stream tunnels. A brook or creek may be easily covered by drifting snow. A fast-running stream will carve out a considerable tunnel, often extending beyond the stream and containing a cave-like air chamber above the stream. Crossing such a stream or, worse yet, traveling up such a stream is as dangerous as crossing a snow-covered crevasse. The snow may not only break and drop you into a cold stream, but may also cave in and trap you. In parts of the western U.S., where snow depths may reach many feet, this is a very real and constant danger.

Crossing a snow-covered stream is as dangerous as crossing a snow-covered crevasse.

Snow-covered stream banks are often undercut by fast-flowing water, giving way when anyone approaches the stream.

In parts of the western United States, where snow depths may reach many feet, cave-ins of snow tunnels are a constant danger for hikers.

If you are traveling in an area where you know a stream to be running or where you suspect one might be, observe the contour of the snow. Frequently, there will be a linear depression running over the streambed where the snow has sagged. Never allow your skis to become parallel over such a depression. If you must cross do so at right angles to the depression and as quickly as possible. Test it first whenever possible. If nothing else, turn a ski pole upside down and stick it into the snow. If it breaks through, detour.

Stream Banks. Free-flowing streams which are not covered by snow can also be dangerous. The banks of streams are frequently undercut by the fast-flowing water, thus presenting a problem when a thirsty traveler approaches the stream. The bank may suddenly give way, resulting in an unexpected slide down into the brook. Ending up soaking wet in the winter with no place to dry off is not only unpleasant but very dangerous, with the threat of instant hypothermia. Should you find yourself suddenly dunked in the drink and the snow is reasonably dry when you climb out, roll in the snow. Snow acts as a sponge and will soak up water from your clothes. It can then be brushed off carrying the water with it. Several treatments like this can dry clothes to a substantial degree. A word of caution: This won't work in *wet* snow!

Brush Piles. Simply stated, brush piles are bushes which have become laden with snow. They act as super snares when some unsuspecting soul walks on top of them. They are less dangerous than maddening, but a little caution will preserve both your temper and dignity.

Snow-covered countryside, often breathtaking, can be danger-ous if the traveler doesn't know what problems to look out for.

Related Reading

Fraser, Colin, *The Avalanche Enigma*. Rand Mc-
Nally and Co., Chicago, IL 1966

Gallagher, *Snowy Torrents—Avalanche Accidents
in the U.S. 1910-1966*, Alta Avalanche Study
Center, Ogden, UT, 1967

La Chappelle, E.R., *The ABC of Avalanche Safety*.
2nd ed., rev., Colorado Outdoor Sports Co.,
Denver, CO, 1970

Williams, Knox, *The Snowy Torrents: Avalanche Accidents in the United States 1967-1971*. Gen.
Tech. Rep. RM-8. U.S. Department of Agriculture Forest Service, 1975

Perla, Ronald I., and Mario Mutinelli, Jr., *Avalanche
Handbook*. U.S. Dept. of Agriculture Handbook
489, 1976

4

Routes, Maps and Compass

Now that we have covered the weather so that you know *when* to travel, and snow conditions and avalanche characteristics so that you know *where not* to go, it is time to discuss *where* and *how* to go. Thousands of summer backpackers and, in many parts of the country, almost as many cross-country skiers get along very well plodding across marked trails and somehow managing not to get into trouble. They have never even looked at the compass they so carefully packed because someone said they should have one handy. And even if they took it out they might be at a loss to know how the fool thing works. There is an old proverb that God takes care of fools and small children. However, there is some doubt about whether this heavenly supervision is extended to skiers and mountaineers. So, if you plan to go ramming about the back country, a few simple basics of navigation are in order.

Common Sense, Sense of Direction and Dead Reckoning

These methods are most unreliable, variable and to some degree based on the emotional state of the individual. It therefore follows that these are the methods frequently chosen by most experienced back country travelers. The key word here is *experienced*, because if you have been around long enough to grow a sixth sense of direction—and this seems the only way to acquire it—then you also are experienced enough to know when the weather is dropping in or you are entering a thick stand of trees and a check with a map and compass is in order. Becoming really good at direction-finding cannot be taught in the formal sense of education; it is developed by practice and observation.

In any case, you take out the map and compass and check your bearings before you get completely lost. Each time you go out on a trip, practice observing the features of the land, the direction of your route and the speed and distance of your travel. Observe the position of the sun. It still rises in the southeast and sets in the southwest. In winter it hangs well to the south. If you're fairly close to the middle of your time zone, shadows point due north at noon, standard time, 1 P.M. daylight savings time. All of these factors and a thousand more go into the complex system of that sixth sense; so practice and observe well.

The Compass

A compass is a magnetized piece of metal placed on a pivot allowing it to turn freely and thereby align itself with the magnetic lines of force of our planet. The earth's magnetic lines of force run north and south, from points near the North and South Poles, known as the magnetic poles. To enable one to read the compass and to establish a point of reference, the north-seeking end of the needle is always marked and a dial is placed around the needle. The dial is divided into degrees and the cardinal directions of north, south, east and west are marked: north 0°, east 90°, south 180°, west 270° and then back to north at 360° or 0°.

Before we get into the use of a compass, there are a few things that must be remembered about magnetic lines of force. First they are bent by strong electrical fields such as those produced by radio transmitters or power transmission lines. The magnetic needle of a compass will also be attracted toward any large metal object. These conditions are easy to watch for, so you need only remember to step a few feet from the car or to put down any metal equipment before using a compass.

A less and more constant source of error is the difference between magnetic north and true north. The magnetic north pole is located a little northwest of Hudson Bay. Your compass will therefore point toward that pole, rather than the true north pole from which the meridians shown on maps are drawn. When working from a map to a compass, you must always take into consideration the difference between north as shown on the map

To obtain your bearings, stand with the compass held horizontally in front of you. Align the compass so that the needle points toward north on the compass. As you face a landmark, sight across the center of the dial. The figure in degrees on the dial is the bearing of the landmark.

and north as shown on the compass. This difference is called the *declination* and is listed in the margin of almost all good maps. The declination is stated in the number of degrees off true north that your compass will read in the area covered by the map. When you are not using a map, but merely using your compass to orient yourself to general landmarks, you need not figure in the declination; accept the compass readings at face value.

Using the Compass

To obtain bearings, stand with the compass held horizontally, squarely in front of you. Align the compass so that the needle points toward north on the dial. As you face an object or landmark, sight across the center of the dial and read the figure in degrees on the dial. This is the bearing of the landmark expressed in degrees.

If you wish to travel to that distant point, all you need do is travel in a straight line on that particular bearing. Stop periodically to check the compass in the same manner to assure that you are maintaining the correct direction of travel. To return to your starting point, either add or subtract 180 degrees from your original bearing and follow the new bearing in the same manner.

When using an orienteering compass such as the Silva System®, these steps are made simpler. The orienteering compass consists of three parts: a magentic needle, a revolving dial and a transparent base plate on which is marked an arrow for direction of travel. When using the Silva, hold the base so that the direction of travel arrow points to the landmark, then turn the dial to match north on the magnetic needle. The point on the dial at the base of the direction of travel arrow will indicate your bearing. To return to your starting point, simply leave the setting the same, but hold the base plate so that the arrow points directly at you and travel in the opposite direction. You may also turn the dial 180 degrees to produce the same effect.

Due to some intervening obstacle, it is not always possible to travel cross-country on a straight line, on a fixed bearing. To maintain your course on the fixed bearing requires some careful attention to detail, but it is really not difficult. Basically there are two methods: right angle travel and triangular travel. When you arrive at an obstacle simply check your bearing and travel exactly 90 degrees from the original bearing, either to the right or to the left. This is easily done with an orienteering compass by sighting across the base plate. When you have traveled far enough to clear the obstacle, return to your original course. Once past the barrier, travel the exact same distance in the direction opposite to your original 90-degree detour.

When right angle detours are too long, a shorter distance can be traveled by triangulation. When a barrier is encountered, determine a course on an angle to the right or left or your original bearing. Note the number of degrees off the original bearing of your new line of march. Travel a fixed distance to a point clear of the obstacle and there take another sighting on your original bearing. Then use an angle the same number of degrees in the opposite direction of your original detour and return the same distance as you did on the first leg of the detour. You will return to a point along the original bearing, clear of the obstacle.

Maps

There are many types of maps available: highway maps, street

When using an orienteering compass, hold the transparent base plate so that the direction of travel arrow points to the landmark, and turn the dial to match north on the magnetic needle. The point on the dial at the base of the direction of travel arrow will indicate your bearing.

maps, nautical charts and many more. Most of these maps are concerned with man-made features and list only such prominent landmarks as rivers and large mountains. They do not, however, show the countours of the land or the natural features, such as springs and small streams. For this information you must consult a *topographic map.** Before leaving your car at the road head, it is a good idea to check a road map to get the general lay of the land and note the direction of major highways or perimeter roads that may surround the area of your trip. However, as topographic maps are the only ones that are useful for cross-country travel, all further discussion in this section will be limited to this kind of map.

To read a map, spread it out before you. Maps are always printed so that north is at the top, south at the bottom, east is to the right and west to the left. A handy way to remember the types of information contained on a map is to break it down into five categories: *description, details, directions, distances and designations.*

*Printed by the U.S. Geological Survey, topographic maps are available in better sporting goods stores or by contacting the USGS in Denver, Colo. 80225 or Washington, D.C. 20242.

Descriptions. This information is listed in the margin of the map. It includes the name of the map, which is usually named for some major landmark or town shown on the map, and the date the map was printed (which is helpful if a road or dam has been built recently). Also listed in the margins are numbers in degrees and minutes and seconds (e.g. 45° 30' 22'') that refer to the latitude and longitude of the land covered by the map. Additional descriptions, such as the map's scale, the magnetic declination for that area, and the names of adjacent maps are also listed.

Details. Details are the symbols used on the map to indicate various features of the landscape as well as man-made features, such as roads, buildings, power lines and the like. Map symbols can be broken down into the following categories:

Man-made Features—Printed in *black* except for major roads which are overprinted in red. These features are the only ones that are not to scale.

Water Features—These features are printed in *blue* and include all bodies of water: swamps, oceans, rivers, ponds and springs.

Vegetation Features—Printed in green, indicate wooded, scrub or orchard areas.

Elevation Features—Printed in *brown* contour lines. Contour lines are imaginary lines drawn along the ground along which every point is at the same height above sea level. The distance in height between the contour lines is called the *contour interval*. The contour interval varies from map to map but is listed in a note at the bottom of each map. At regular intervals, a darker more prominent contour line will be drawn. Somewhere along this line the elevation above sea level will be listed. Elevations of the summits of prominent peaks or other features are also listed. These numbers appear in black for peaks and in blue for water features.

Direction. As already indicated, north is at the top of the map. The simplest way to determine the direction from one point on

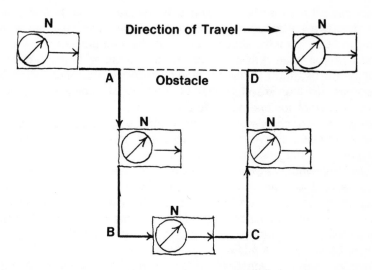

To travel around an obstacle using right angles, use the back edge of the orienteering compass base plate for sighting. The distance traveled from A to B must equal the distance from C to D.

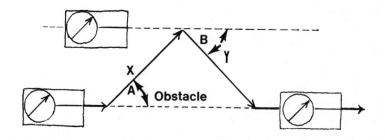

To travel around an obstacle using two angles, use the compass dial as a protractor. Don't change the bearing setting. Determine the angle of travel needed to clear the obstacle, and then check your original bearing. Using the same angle as before, but in the opposite direction, return an equal distance to your original line of travel. Angle A must equal angle B, and distance X must equal distance Y.

the map to another is by using a transparent, 360-degree protractor. Draw a straight line connecting your starting point with
0° or 360° directly above (north) of the starting point. Where
the line you have drawn intersects the perimeter of the protractor is the bearing of your destination from your starting point. If
you wish to then travel to that destination by compass, remember to *correct for the magnetic declination.*

Distance. The scale varies on different topographic maps, but is
easy to measure from the scale shown on the map using a piece
of paper or the edge of the base plate of an orienteering compass. Remember, in figuring distance, to take into consideration
the vertical distance as well. A route with a lot of uphill travel
can be miles longer on tired legs. Try to relate time to distance
and keep this dimension in mind.* It's something that only your
experience can teach you, so don't bite off more than you can
chew before you've gained some experience.

Designations. Designations refer to anything written on the
maps. It can be anything from the name of a town or mountain
to a boundary, like a county line. There may also be elevation
figures, bench marker notations and other control data for
surveyors.

Marked in red at intervals across the top and bottom of each
map are such figures as R 19 E. These are range lines which
extend north and south across the map and are used to subdi-
vide each map. The same type of red figures extending at intervals down the sides of the map indicate east-west or town lines,
i.e., T 6 N. The basis for these numbers is determined by a
base line running either north or south through an established
point.

The base lines and their fixed points are the starting points
for all surveys. Hence, a notation of R 19 E means that you are
19 range lines east of a north-south base line. The figure of T 6
N means you are six townlines north of an east-west base line.
All lines, range or town, are six miles apart. Hence, when taken
together they form a square six miles by six miles, or 36 square
miles in area. Such an area is referred to as a township. Each
township is designated by the range and town lines which cross
at its center. Hence, township R 19 E (range 19 east) and T 6
N (township 6 north).

---

*A speed of one mile per hour can be considered a safe estimate in unfa-
miliar terrain or when traveling with new companions. Actual speeds on cross-
country skis probably will greatly exceed this.

Each township is also marked off by dashed red lines into 36 squares. These are referred to as sections. Each section contains 640 acres or one square mile. However, these sections in rough, mountainous country may not be square or even contain 640 acres. On the map the sections in each township are numbered in red from 1 to 36. Therefore, if you wished to note a given location on a map you might describe it as section 32, R 19 E, T 6 N on a specific map.

For the purpose of further division, each section is divided into quarters by north-south/east-west lines. Each quarter is again divided by another pair of lines. Hence, the description of the northwest corner of the southeast quarter of section 32 R 19 E T 6 N on a specific map.

Such designations are, of course, important to a surveyor, but if you have to tell a rescue team the location of a downed buddy, that is the way they will want to hear it spelled out. There is a second somewhat more detailed system of determining locations on these maps. The system is known as the Universal Transverse Mercator grid—or UTM. The lines for this grid are shown in blue and divide the map into 1000-meter grids. The figures noted in black along the side margins of the map appear as numbers such as 42 65, which means 42 65000 meters north. The next number north from this would be 42 66 or 42 66000 meters north. By dividing the distance between each of these lines into 10 equal segments you can pinpoint a spot down to 100 meters. The marks at the top and bottom of the map are similarly noted with the exception of an east or west designation.

Hence, by carefully working with the UTM grid you could pinpoint a location on a given map to within about 50 meters.

This discussion may seem pretty technical and rather absurd to try and follow, but may I suggest you obtain a U.S. Geological Survey map and do some work with it. Look for the designations I have mentioned around the border of the map and work out various locations on that map. These systems will not help you a great deal in field travel, but should the occasion ever arise when a technical description of a given point on the map is required, these are the systems you will likely be asked to use.

Map Interpretation

Once you have a working knowledge of the symbols and designations on a topographic map, you must put them together and make some sense out of what you see. One of the primary areas of concern will be to determine the amount of hill climbing or descending you may be in for on any given trip. This is done by using the brown contour lines. First check the margin of the map and find out what the contour interval is for the map. The closer the lines are together, the steeper the slope. If a large number of lines merge, you can expect to find a large cliff.

To determine whether you would be traveling uphill or downhill, note the numbers located along the darker contour lines. If, as you proceed in a given direction, you find the numbers getting larger, then expect a rise in the land. Concentric lines indicate a hill. In the case of a depression, you would see concentric lines but with small lines extending inward from each circular line.

Another clue is that if a stream is noted on the map the contour lines often have a small V at the stream. The bottom of the V always points uphill.

Areas with green overprinted are wooded areas, while areas left white are open. Occasionally in the mountains you might note contour lines in blue on a mountain side; these indicate a glacier.

As a study guide, you should obtain a topographic map of an area in which you plan to be spending some time. Study it and observe the various notations on the map, trying to visualize the landscape you would expect to encounter on a given hike. It is always best to try with a map of a country which is familiar to you. That way you can cross-check your map reading skill.

Traveling

Now that the fundamentals of maps and compass are in hand, the application of this information to actual field experiences is of foremost importance.

There are a few general points worth remembering. A quick look at a good world map will tell you that most mountain ranges run north and south. Because there seems little point in running roads along the summits of mountain chains, man has built his roads running across mountains. Therefore, most major mountain roads run east and west. In wider mountain chains such as the Rockies, there are a few roads going north and south along the floors of valleys. But as a general rule, major routes through mountains are east-west roads. In the western United States the mountains generally have a steep slope and a gentle slope. This is especially true of the Sierras, where the western slope is gentle and the eastern slope is very steep. In the eastern states, where the mountains are older and more worn by weather, the mountains tend to be rounded and more equally sloped.

Before you leave for your trip, check the area out on both a topographic and road map. On the road map, determine the area and its boundaries. How far is it to the next highway? Where is the nearest town and, in case of trouble, where is the nearest help to be found? On the topographic map of the area that you intend to visit, make a note of the direction of the prevailing wind. If you do not know this, check with the local weather station or ranger station. From this information you will know which is the lee slope with its heavier snow build up.

It is also helpful to check on what roads in the vicinity will be plowed and which are closed in the winter. Knowing this, you should determine where to leave your auto. Then with the destination in mind, lay out the safest and easiest route for your travel. Check the compass bearings of the area. If your trip is off the north side of a main road, no matter how twisted up you might become, all you need to do to find the road again is travel south. In addition to roads, natural barriers are also important to observe. If there is a major river or stream in the area or a chain of high ridges, keep in mind their position and direction in relation to other land features.

Planning your route can be a difficult task. Your plans must always remain flexible and allow for changes in the field. You are there to enjoy yourself in the safest possible manner. So the best solution is to know the country well. For this purpose nothing can equal summer travel, but when this is not practical you must establish a route from other means. Summer trails and unplowed back roads shown on topographic maps are good features to start with. Remember, however, these are *summer routes*. In winter, trail markings may not be visible or the route may cross the face of a steep hill which would pose a serious avalanche danger. Trails along a narrow ledge can be quite safe in the summer but impassable in the winter. Do not blindly follow summer trails just because they are there. Frozen rivers and lakes form a large portion of the routes for winter travel in some parts of the country, especially in the northern Great Lakes region. Traveling over such routes requires special attention to possible ice hazards buried deep under winter snows. The location of inlets to lakes may be of utmost importance in such instances.

A great deal can be learned by carefully studying topographic maps, especially about the contour of the land. By studying contour lines you can pick the easiest grade or avoid traversing steep hillsides. Waterways and lakes which may be invisible under the snow are shown, as are the wooded areas. As important as what maps do show is what they do not show.

There is, for example, no way to determine just how dense a wooded area shown on a map actually may be. You might encounter a stand of widely dispersed old trees, or you could run smack into a mass of regrowth or slash brush that would take a tank to penetrate. Maps show streams, but often fail to indicate the depth of the stream bed. It could be only a matter of a few inches, or up to 40 feet with steep banks. Rock formations are not indicated either. A slope which appears to be moderate on a map may, in reality, be a mass of boulders, ledges and outcroppings higher than a house.

It is also a good idea to remember that maps show land features and can make no record of such variable conditions as snow cover. A lake and a flat field look pretty much the same in the winter with a few feet of snow covering them. But the snow on the lake may be concealing a layer of thin ice. Of course, the snow cover is not just snow. It changes from day to day—even hour to hour—often requiring major route correction. Such factors could never be incorporated into a map. So experience and caution seem to be the only answer.

In the Great Lakes region and east across the northern states and Canada, the land is flat and often heavily wooded. No mountain peaks or ridge lines break the horizon as navigation aids and one can often see only a few yards at a time.

In such areas, country orientation can be a special sort of headache. Land features are not easily identified and the country can seem to stretch forever. If lost in such terrain, it is far more difficult to reorient yourself. Here the map becomes secondary to the compass and you must constantly maintain your bearings.

To aid you in your route selection in a new area, a quick review of the local geology and weather patterns, as well as the regional flora, are in order. Remember the land features you encounter are the results of previous geological activity in the area. In valleys or plains with deep top soil, streams etch deep beds, while in mountain meadows where the soil is only inches thick, stream beds tend to be shallow. In the older mountain ranges of the eastern states, sharp ledges and cliffs are less common and the mountains are more rounded than in the western states. Such information can often be gleaned from a guide book or by talking with someone who has been through the country. But whatever the source, always check further than just the surface of the topographical map. Consider the following points as you plot your route:

Safety—Avoid danger zones such as avalanches and thin ice. Allow a safety margin of time to account for unexpected delays or route changes.

Ease of Travel—Try to make any ascends as gradual as possible. Pace yourself so as not to become overtired, and allow for fatigue. Do not press for difficult goals late in the day.

Shelter and Evacuation Routes—Keep such routes in mind in the event that they become needed. That is no time to have to figure things out.

Scenery—Plan your route to give yourself the most enjoyment possible. Just getting someplace fast can be accomplished better in a car or on a snowmobile!

With all this information you should have a fairly accurate mental picture of the country through which you will be traveling. When you arrive at your starting point, take time and check your compass bearings. Orient yourself to the features you have checked on the map, so that the map concept becomes a reality as you look at the land.

As you travel along the predetermined compass bearing, take time at rest stops or at locations with good views to shoot a compass bearing on some major land feature. For example, if you should be traveling on a true north on a bearing of 0°,with a major peak which you will be traveling past off to your right (east), take occasional compass sightings onto the top of the peak. Note the degrees from your line of march. With your line of march drawn along the map, if your sighting should indicate 45°, then draw a line from the top of the peak to the line of your march, on a bearing of 45°. Where the lines cross is very close to where you will be standing.

If your line of march is unknown but you are able to identify

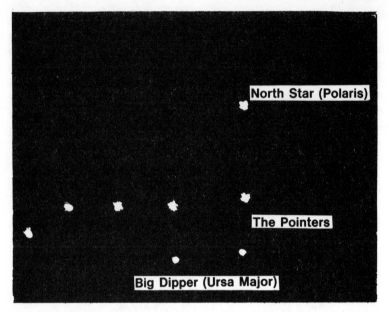

If you need to determine direction on a clear night, the most convenient directional check is the North Star (Polaris), which is located almost directly above the North Pole and always stays within 2½ degrees of true north.

at least two major land features and can get a sighting off each, extend lines on the map at those compass bearings. Where the two lines cross is again approximately where you are. The more methodical you are while taking sightings and accommodating for the magnetic declination, the more accurate you will be in obtaining your exact location.

When working with maps and compass, there are several aids that will make your job much easier. First, the angle of declination, which is noted in the bottom margin of the map, can be extended as a penciled line across the entire map. When you are in the field with the map laid out in front of you, turn it so that your magnetic line points to magnetic north as shown by your compass. With the map so aligned with magnetic north, make all sightings. You can forget about adding or subtracting the magnetic declination. This is possible because you have aligned the map with the compass before you have taken any bearings.

Second, in bad weather the last thing that you'll need is a soggy map. A clear plastic map case is most helpful. This can be either a commercially manufactured case of simply a map folded inside a plastic bag. Some people have even used protective sprays right on their maps with good results.

In the final analysis, it is nearly impossible to learn how to use a map and compass without practice. To become proficient in the field takes a great deal of practice, and even some of the old-timers get their bearings twisted once in a while. But if you exercise great caution and practice, your efforts will be rewarded.

If you need to determine direction on a clear night, the most convenient directional check is the North Star (Polaris). It is located almost directly above the North Pole and always stays within 2-½ degrees of true north. It is a fairly bright star and can best be located by sighting along the two stars at the outer rim of the Big Dipper (Ursa Major).

A rough estimate of direction can be made during the day using the sun's location and checking the time. Rising in the east and setting in the west, the sun will always remain to the south during the winter. At noon, the sun should lie well to the south. The moon also has the same pattern of rising and setting, but it has an erratic time cycle. As a result, it is best to check whether the moon resting near the horizon is going up or down.

There is another method of determining direction by the use of the sun. First, in a sunny area, place a stick vertically into the ground (snow). Note the shadow it casts and mark the tip of the shadow. Wait about 15 minutes until the shadow has moved. Mark the new tip of the shadow. Draw a line from your first mark through the second mark and for about one foot beyond. Stand with the toe of your *left* foot at the first mark and the toe of your *right* foot at the end of the line—you are facing north!

Related Reading

Kjellstrom, Bjorn, *Be Expert With Map and Compass,* American Orienteering Service, La Porte, IN, 1967

U.S. Army, *Map Reading.* U.S. Army, FM-21-26, 1965

Disley, John, *Orienteering.* The Stackpole Co., Harrisburg, PA, 1967

Humphrey, Vernon W., and Stroup, Theodore G., *The Orienteeering Handbook.* U.S. Army Infantry School, Ft. Benning, GA, 1971

U.S. Geological Survey, *Reading U.S. GS Maps.* U.S. Geological Survey Map Sales, Bldg. 41, Denver Federal Center., Denver, CO 80225

U.S. Geological Survey, *State Index to Topographic Maps.* U.S. Geological Survey Map Sales

5

Equipment

In this section we will be discussing some of the pros and cons of different types of equipment. There are also a few suggestions about some minimal equipment—items that should always be carried. As a general rule, good equipment that is taken care of will give the user the best possible wear and is in the long run the least expensive. So when shopping, study the products well and get a good cross section of advice on the various brands that are available.

Clothing

The function of clothing is to keep you warm and protect you from the elements: wind, rain, snow and sun. At the same time, clothing should not tire you or impede your movements. Keeping these points in mind, rather than how stylish or sexy a particular outfit looks, is a good starting point.

There is usually no warm lodge to duck into if the weather drops in or you need a rest, so leave the fast clothes for the Alpine skiing crowd. The amount of warmth retained by clothes is directly proportional to the amount of warm air trapped within the clothes. Also, it is important to note that clothing loses its ability to retain heat when it is wet, either from sweat or external moisture. Wool is the exception to this rule; even when wet it will retain a large proportion of its warmth. Down clothing does not have this property; it is useless when wet.

As previously mentioned, some of the new synthetic fabrics such as Polar Guard® and Fiber Fill II®, while bulky, do offer good protection from cold even when wet. Used as stuffing for bulky jackets and sleeping bags, these materials are a good breakthrough. However, it is too bulky and too warm for rapid travel on Nordic skiis.

Cotton absorbs moisture and becomes damp and clings. It loses nearly all of its heat retaining quality when wet, hence should not be used extensively in the wardrobe.

Several layers of lighter clothes are warmer than a single heavy garment because they trap more air. This multilayered dress also allows you to shed a layer or two to avoid overheating when traveling. For this reason, it is also a good idea to wear clothes that can be opened down the front. On warm days a short uphill run can generate all the heat you can handle. The last thing you want to do is end up with sweat-soaked clothes. A sweater or parka that can't be opened down the front can become quite a sweatbox. However, such clothing can be valuable on cold days as it does not furnish any openings for the wind to enter and cool you off.

Waterproof garments worn during exercise prevent moisture from escaping. Perspiration can build up and make you wetter than could the weather that you're trying to protect yourself from. Tight-fitting clothes tend to inhibit movement and cut circulation, neither of which are desirable qualities. Clothes that chafe or tend to bunch up in sensitive areas are also to be avoided.

With these thoughts in mind, plan your clothing around a multilayered system that can be adjusted in the field to provide maximum protection against varied weather conditions. The following suggestions are to be taken as generally applicable, but should be augmented with heavier clothing for very cold weather or high altitude trips.

Underwear. Cotton serves well. It is soft, comfortable and easily washed. Weight varies greatly, from light to heavy thermal types. The fish net variety is favored by many because it traps a good deal of air while still preventing the buildup of sweat. It is quite cool on a hot day when a shirt is unbuttoned down the front. Wool underwear is unquestionably very warm and maintains its protection even when damp; its drawback is that it is very irritating to some people with sensitive skin.

There are, however, several brands of super-soft wool underwear available, some being produced in the fish net variety. These are probably the best answer for people with sensitive skin. But as far as cost goes, gold would be cheaper!

Pants. Only one fabric is really acceptable—wool. The weight of the fabric can be varied but it should always be a tight weave. The wool may also be protected by a coat of sprayed-on waterproofing. Most cross-country skiers find that knickers give the best freedom of movement. An inexpensive pair of knickers can be produced by buying a pair of wool pants from an Army surplus store. With a little doctoring they can be cut off into very fine knickers. A coat of waterproof spray will top off the job. Nordic ski racers favor very light polyester knickers that are highly elastic. These do not overheat the racer and afford the maximum range of movement. For the ski tourer, however, they would likely be too cool and not afford adequate protection. In bad weather or around the camp in the evening, warmup pants or powder pants may be added over the knickers for protection, but for general travel these are too warm.

Shirts and Sweaters. Over an undershirt, a good wool shirt works well. On warm days, pull it out of your trousers and wear the sleeves and front open to allow air to circulate. Closed up and tucked in, it is a very warm garment. A bulky knit wool sweater works well as the next layer; on warmer days it can be stuffed in your pack to put on during lunch breaks or rest stops.

Jacket or Parka. Some form of windbreaker over the sweater is advisable. A windproof jacket that opens down the front and has an attached hood is a good bet. It is also helpful if it sheds snow and does not absorb moisture; this will keep you dry when you fall. On very warm days such a jacket can be worn with only a T-shirt under it. It is always advisable to wear some form of protective outer garment. T-shirts and halter tops do not protect you from painful scrapes, icy snow or the burning effects of ultraviolet rays, to say nothing of the instant hypothermia or shock caused by lying injured and unclothed in the snow.

Down Clothing. A good down jacket shuld be carried in your pack, preferably in a waterproof bag. At night around the camp or in case of emergency bivouac, it can be indispensable. Remember, however, if the down gets wet, it is useless. Also, a down jacket is too warm to wear while traveling, except in the most extreme conditions. Jackets which utilize synthetic fibers may be good substitutes for down. Careful consideration of the probability of getting wet, as well as cost factors, are in order before you buy a jacket.

Rain Gear. Another item to have in a pack is a poncho or cagoule. These are vital, should the weather turn bad and you encounter rain. These items can also be used for emergency shelter construction, especially the poncho. Rain pants are also very helpful, both in rain and wet snow.

Boots and Socks. Because we are talking about foot travel, no item should be approached with greater care and more consideration. Proper fit is essential. A point to remember is that in cross-country skiing the action of the foot tends to push it forward in the boot; be sure you have boots that are long enough to prevent your toes from being jammed into the end of the boot. This can cause a loss of toenail and much pain. Ill-fitting boots or chafing socks are the main cause of blisters and a main source of first-aid problems on the trail. Cross-country boots are available in both high and low-cut models. Which you choose is a matter of personal preference. The lower cut models are lighter, more flexible and are used by racers for speed. The higher cut types offer better ankle support for downhill runs, are warmer, and are used for more rugged mountaineering conditions. Wool socks are also important; usually a double layer works best, again for warmth. But it is essential to carry an extra dry pair or two in your pack. A coat of waterproofing spray also works well on the tops of the socks, which are exposed to snow. The extra pair of dry socks can double as a pair of mittens if the need should arise.

Gaiters. These are water-resistant protectors that are worn around the ankles and serve to keep snow out of the boots. They are available in many lengths and materials. Again, personal preference comes into play, but some form of gaiter should be worn to keep socks and boots dry.

Hats and Headwear. The body can lose an enormous amount of heat through an unprotected head. Therefore, some form of hat is necessary and should be used on all but the very best days. A Balaclava is an excellent choice because it can convert to a full face protector as well as a general cap. Whatever headgear you choose, be sure it can come down to protect your ears, the back of your neck and the temples.

Gloves and Mittens. Mittens are warmer than gloves, and whether or not you wish to wear them, at least one extra pair of mitts should be carried in your pack. All sorts of gloves and mittens are on the market. You should carry a warm pair that are reasonably water-repellent and snow-repellent and which also cover the wrists. Another small item that is good to have in the pack is a pair of glove liners. These are made of cotton, wool, silk or synthetic fabric. They are very thin and light, which will allow you to work easily with cold equipment. A pair of long, water-repellent nylon over mittens is another good item. They are worn over jacket sleeves, protecting from wind. These mittens work well to keep out snow if you are digging a snow cave.

Miscellaneous Items. A wide variety of other items may be added: Scarves, neck and chest protectors, down booties and boot covers. The list can go on and on. But the items listed above are the basics and should be considered first. The other things you may wish to pack along as personal preference and comfort decree.

Eye Protection

This is an *absolute must!* Ultraviolet rays, increased by the reflection from the snow, can cook your eyes. A good pair of sun glasses are fine for general usage. But for high altitude work or long periods of exposure in large snow fields, additional protection may be required. Shields which reduce peripheral light may be added. Also, many types of goggles are available and should be considered.

Packs

You may have noticed that several references to a pack have slipped in from time to time. Well, unless you are racing, some form of pack is essential. For the day tripper this can be a minimum day-pack or small rucksack that should be large enough to carry a few items of clothing, a small first-aid kit, a repair kit, your lunch and a camera. There are few other items that a hiker should always carry; these will be discussed later.

Day-packs are either of the frameless or internal-frame variety. The same pack doubles well for the summmer day hike or as a lunch and and camera bag or an assault pack on a rock climb.

For more extended trips involving overnight stays you will need a larger pack. In this category there seems to be a mind-boggling assortment of equipment available. As a rule, try to get a pack that is large enough to do what you want, but not too large because you're going to have to carry it, loaded. Also try for one which is versatile. Highly specialized equipment is great but it has narrow application and can be expensive.

Determine your needs and try to find a pack that will best suit you for size and number of pockets. Outside attachments for equipment and skis are important extras to consider. Basically, for skiing purposes, a pack should fit close to the body and its weight should be carried as close to the hips as possible. It should also allow freedom of movement and be easy to put on and take off. There are many types of support systems for packs, such as the following:

Monocoque—Has no frame and depends on its shape and load to distribute the weight. These packs fit very close to the body and conform best to your contours, if packed correctly.

Internal Stays—Have metal stays sewn into them. The stays may be of several types; X-Stays or European Y-Frames are the most popular. These bags comprise the rucksack variety of pack. They conform well to the body and are quite comfortable.

Perimeter Frame—Somewhat more rigid but lighter and closer fitting than the standard frame pack. They have a tubular frame surrounding the bag and the straps are attached to the frame.

Pack Frame—The load carriers. No other pack can equal the volume or weight capacity of these packs. They have the disadvantage of riding high and far away from the body, which can easily swing a skier off balance. The top cross bar of the frame has a nasty habit of clouting one behind the head when you fall. Also, they are the best pack for most summer backpacking trips.

Whichever pack you choose, there are a few simple rules to be followed in packing the bag for travel. First, be sure the load is balanced. Heavier items should be centered near the spine to prevent you from being spun around when turning. Hard or sharp items should be packed toward the rear, away from the carrier. The weight should be low for downhill skiing, slightly higher for uphill travel.

It's a good idea to place items in clear plastic bags. This way your pack is neat and orderly and your gear is kept dry, while remaining visible. It saves a lot of poking around in the pack for smaller items. The plastic bags also double as dirty clothes or garbage bags on the way out. Equipment you will need during travel should be carried in outer pockets or near the top of the

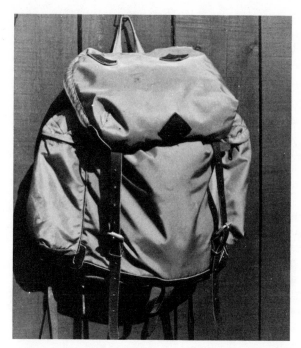

The hiker's day-pack should be large enough to carry a few items of clothing, a small first-aid kit, a repair kit, lunch and a camera.

pack. Stashing an extra packet of matches in a couple of different places is always a good idea. Matches should either be stored in water-tight metal containers or removed from your pack, except when the pack is in use. When traveling or in storage they constitute a major fire hazard.

Tents

Nothing can equal a fine quality mountaineering tent. There is also probably no such thing as a perfect tent, so what we shall do here is examine the features of tents and discuss the merits of each. Then, within the limits of your piggy bank, you should get the best one possible. A word of caution: Plastic tube tents do not work well in the summer and are entirely out of place in the winter. As an emergency shelter, they may be carried along on day trips, but beyond this they should be avoided.

Because it is usually both the most expensive and the heaviest piece of your equipment, great care should be taken in choosing the proper tent for your needs. Remember the many functions of a tent: to shelter you from the wetness of a storm or fog, to retain warmth in cold weather, and to shield you from wind, heat and insects. With these in mind, shop carefully before buying.

Fabrics. Cotton has many advantages. Properly treated cotton repels moisture as well as coated nylon; hence, no fly is needed. It will also absorb moisture from the inside of a tent and pass it to the outside. Good cotton such as Wyncol Fabric is also highly wind resistant. The chief disadvantages of cotton and the main reasons it has been almost totally replaced by nylon as a tent fabric are its greater weight, its lower tear resistance and its tendency to mildew.

Nylon tent fabrics commonly available are nylon taffeta and ripstop nylon. Taffeta is heavier (2.5 to 3.5 ounces) and more abrasion-proof, but less resistant to tearing. Ripstop is lighter (1.9 ounces) and highly tear resistant, but can be damaged by abrasion.

Nylon is not waterproof and does not hold waterproofing well. It must therefore be coated with a polymer, polyurethane, or vi-

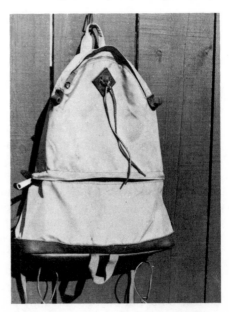

The teardrop-shaped rucksack comfortably carries gear close to the body.

The framed backpack transfers most of the pack's total weight to the pelvic girdle, which is the body part best designed to support weight.

nyl coating. This coating can, under prolonged weathering, crack, peel off and hence require recoating. As nylon does not swell when wet, the stitching holes may have to be sealed with a special compound to prevent leaks along seams.

Condensation is a problem with all nylon; coated nylon will not breathe at all and creates an exceptional condensation problem. Therefore, nylon tents must be well vented and are best constructed with an uncoated canopy. Since a nylon tent is not water resistant, it must be protected by a fly, a coated nylon sheet stretched over the tent with an air space left between the walls. It sheds water while allowing the uncoated tent to breathe and prevents condensation buildup.

In addition to the tent fly, the floor and lower portion of the canopy should be coated to prevent moisture from seeping in from the ground or snow.

In practice, because of its high abrasion resistance, the floor and fly are often made from coated taffeta, while the canopy is ripstop nylon. This combination is found on many of the better tents. Tents with coated canopies are available but are sweat boxes in the summer and become lined with frost in the winter.

The other great problem with nylon is its flammability. It is prone to melt at high temperatures and is very vulnerable to fire.

Back view of backpack frame.

Tent Construction. Seams are a weak point in any fabric and should be carefully examined in any tent. The strongest seams are flat fell seams. They should be doublestitched with the stitching evenly spaced using 8 to 10 stitches per inch.

In checking out a tent, look for adequate reinforcing at stress points. The best reinforcing is an additional layer of nylon or, better yet, nylon webbing, stitched around the attachment of tie-down loops and other stress points.

Naturally, in any tent all entrances and vents should be covered with nylon mosquito netting. You should be able to close this netting completely. Insects are no problem in the winter, but then a tent is not a winter-only item.

Ventilation is vital to the tent sleeper, and even more so if you should ever try to cook in the tent. When cooking there must always be cross ventilation, preferably at the top of the tent, just under the ridge line where the vent is protected by the fly.

A word of caution: No one in his right mind would crawl into a plastic bag, tie the ends together, and go to sleep. This is exactly what you would be doing if you slept in a coated tent or tube tent with the doors and vents closed.

Entrances used in tents are of two types: the triangular door closed by a zipper and the tunnel. Under winter conditions, even the best plastic zipper can stick, which might cause some serious exit problems in the morning. However, the triangular door is much more comfortable for movement in and out of the tent. The tunnel, having no zipper, cannot fail—even in the worst weather—and it affords a weather-proof way to crawl in and out of the tent. The best possible arrangement is to have both types of entrance, one at each end of the tent. This allows a winter-proof entrance and good cross ventilation on hot summer nights. Such a tunnel can also be rolled together with a second tent, making a weather-tight seal between the tents.

Poles form the skeleton that supports your tent and are a vital part of its construction. They are usually jointed aluminum. The better ones have a length of shock cord running down the middle of the tube to hold them together and prevent a section from becoming lost.

Several systems of poles are in use; the simplest and lightest is an I-pole. This is a single pole in the center of each end of the tent. Its disadvantage is that it takes up room and obstructs the entrance. The second configuration in wide use is the A-frame; the poles run down sleeves at the corners of the tent. This system, while adding the weight of an extra pair of poles, allows for greater freedom at the entrances and keeps the canopy much tighter.

Exoskeletons are used in several tents now on the market. These employ an exterior framework of poles, with the canopy suspended from shock cords. In some systems the poles are flexible (often fiber glass) and are inserted into sleeves in the canopy. These rely on the spring action of the poles to keep the walls tight. Any exoskeletal tent will support itself without additional guy lines, but they still must be nailed down against the wind. Their disadvantages: they tend to flap in the wind more than triangular tents and have a heavier, more complex system of poles. In any case, remember that in the event of an avalanche, tent poles can be used as probes.

For winter use, a cook hole, which is a zippered trap door in the floor of the tent, is very helpful. It is really a must if you plan to cook inside your tent. The snow is dug out under the trap door and the stove is set down in the pit, protecting the tent from damage. Vestibules are often available, either built in or added on. They form a sheltered area for storage of equipment and protect the inside of the tent from weather. Some of the better tents have small pouches sewn along the inside of the canopy to hold small items. If your tent does not have such pockets, you might consider adding them. Building them with mosquito netting would even allow access to their contents without groping.

Under very cold conditions, a frost liner may be necessary. This is a cotton sheet hung inside of the tent to catch condensation, preventing the occupants from being snowed on all night. An acceptable liner can be fabricated at home from light cotton or cheesecloth.

Care of Tents. Whichever tent you choose, take good care of it. Tents will last a long time and give many years of good service if given proper care. Do not wear boots inside the tent and avoid stepping on the tent when setting it up. Never place sharp items on the floor; you might sit on them and cut the fabric.

Keep the tent as clean as possible. Stove fuel is very destructive to nylon, especially to some of the coatings used on floors and flies. Keep fire well away from the tent; if you cook inside, check the walls for overheating. An extra measure I use is to carry plastic tarp the same size as the floor of my tent and spread this on the ground under the tent. It is remarkable how many fine holes and scuff marks these plastic tarps have accumulated, compared to the total absence of any in the floor of my tent.

When you arrive home from a trip, open the tent and air it out, drying it thoroughly before repacking. It should be stored in a cool, dry place out of the sun. Nylon rots with prolonged exposure to the sun. This is not a problem when the tent is in use, but if stored in direct sunlight it could be a large factor. Storing it on a hanger in a closet is an excellent way to keep it dry, odor-free and away from light.

Sleeping Bags

Pound for pound there is nothing that can equal a good quality goose-down sleeping bag for warmth. However, the construction of the bag can make a great difference in the amount of warmth you obtain for the weight of the down you have available. It is worth noting that the rules for down clothing apply equally to down bags. If the bag gets wet, it is useless.

Sleeping bags are usually covered with nylon, which is highly flammable and quite fragile, so take care of them. The warmth provided by the down depends on the amount of loft or fluffiness in the material. So when putting up your camp, take the bag out of the stuff sack and allow it to fluff up before bedtime.

The down in the bag is enclosed in tubes. The manner of construction for these tubes greatly affects the warmth of the bag. Bags with the seams sewn-through use a cheap form of construction, produce cold spots, and should be avoided. The slant tube construction uses a long, sloping baffle between the inner and outer shell of the bag. This produces an overlapping effect and allows the down to expand more than with other modes of construction and is therefore warmest, for a given amount of down. Box construction uses a vertical baffle between the inner and outer shell. It is not as warm as the slant tube and is used on less expensive bags. Overlapping tube construction used on heavier bags, required for extreme winter conditions, is warmer but requires more down, more fabric and, of course, is more expensive.

Aside from the tube construction of a bag, it is also important to determine whether a space filler cut or a differential cut has been used. In the space filler bag, the inner shell is made the same size as the outer shell. This allows the inner shell to settle around the body, filling the space inside the bag. The differential cut is one in which the inner shell is smaller than the outer shell, forming concentric shells and allowing for greater loft of the down, hence more warmth.

The chart below indicates the thickness in inches of down needed to maintain comfort when sleeping. Remember this is an average; some people sleep a lot colder than others.

	WIND SPEED MPH				
Temperature F°	**0**	**10**	**20**	**30**	**40**
40	1½	1¾	2	2	2¼
30	1¾	2	2½	2½	3
20	2	2½	2¾	3	3¼
10	2¼	2¾	3	3¼	3½
0	2½	3	3½	3¾	4
-10	2¾	3¼	3¾	4	4¼
-20	3	3¾	4	4¼	4½

The shape of a bag is also subject to personal preference. The mummy or modified mummy bags afford ample room and are less heavy and bulky than the rectangle or barrel-shaped bags.

Much recent work has been done in the development of the synthetic fiber bag using Fiber Fill II® and Polar Guard®. These bags, which are non-allergins for those who are allergic to feathers, offer a good deal of warmth when wet, are less expensive than down, and are somewhat easier to care for. Their drawback is bulk. They take up considerably more room in a pack than down bags. When shopping for one of these bags, the same amount of care should be exercised as when shopping for a good down bag. Workmanship and construction vary greatly from brand to brand.

Insulating Ground Pads

During the winter, the air in an air mattress gets too cold for comfort. A bit harder on the hips but much warmer are foam pads. They are so much warmer that they should be considered a must. There are many varieties of pads: air cap pads, open-cell and closed-cell pads, covered pads, thick and thin pads. When all is said and done, however, the closed-cell foam pad is the best. They do not absorb water and can be used to sit directly on the snow during a lunch break. But more important, they give the most warmth at night for sleeping. Into this category fall the well-known Ensolite and Blu-Foam pads. A thickness of ⅜ inch or thicker is best for winter use. A full-length pad is essential for winter camping. For day packers a small piece of Ensolite, large enough to sit on, makes a handy item at lunch time. Also, several of these small pads from different members of the party can be laid out to protect an accident victim. Other types of pads are either too bulky, absorb moisture or are not well suited for winter usage.

Stoves

Here is a subject suitable for a fine debate. Every old-timer has his opinion as to which is the best stove on the market. The only objective way to handle the subject is to list the various types and some of the pros and cons for each. Then you will have to make up your own mind. The perfect stove has not been invented, so if you are an inventor you might start to work.

White Gas Stoves (Optimus, Primus, Svea). These stoves produce an excellent, long-lasting source of heat. White gas is the

Metal cookware, light and durable, is standard for most outdoors-people.

most commonly used stove fuel, readily available in the U.S. White gas is highly volatile; the pressure of the heated fuel is adequate to force the fuel into the burner without pumping except in extreme cold. As a rule most of these stoves should be insulated from the snow to maintain proper pressure while in use. Their drawback is that they are difficult to start. All must be primed, which can be accomplished by using fuel or some paste-type fire starter. Because of its volatility the fuel is very flammable. If spilled it can be ignited by a spark or an open flame. Hence the stove should never be filled inside a tent and should be used in a tent only with great caution. With these or any liquid fuel stoves, fuel must be carried in a leakproof container, lest it spill in the pack and damage food supplies or clothing. Being quite volatile, it does quickly evaporate from fabric but will damage waterproofing. Such stoves should be equiped with a pressure pump for winter starting.

Kerosene (Optimus 96L, OOL, 48). Kerosene is the most readily available and least expensive fuel on a world-wide basis. It has a very low volatility and its vapor will not ignite at normal room temperatures. As a result the stove must be preheated by a separate fuel before use. The low volatility is an advantage in cold weather operation; the stove can safely be used inside a tent. The stove can also be set directly on the snow during operation. Care must be used, however, to prevent leakage of fuel into your pack; it will not evaporate and destroys food and damages other equipment.

Butane Cartridges (Bleuet). Butane cartridges are the most expensive and heaviest fuel to carry. They are also the easiest to use; just turn the valve and hold a lighted match to the burner. There is no danger of fuel leakage, so the stoves can be used inside tents. As long as the fuel cartridges are kept above the freezing point, which can be a problem, these stoves work well at low temperatures and high altitudes. Their disadvantages lie in their somewhat lower heat output and the fact that the cartridges cannot be removed until they are completely empty. This presents a disposal problem and empty cartridges stink when carried around in a pack.

Propane Cartridges. These are the newest and least tested of all the stoves. Their use cost and heat production is similar to butane. The advantage seems to be in the ability to disconnect the cartridge before it is totally empty. A word of caution: When disconnecting any type of cartridge, be very careful. Compressed gas, when it squirts out of a can, is extremely cold and will freeze tissue if it comes in contact with the skin, causing instant frostbite.

There are other types of stoves on the market. Those listed above are a sample of the most common types currently in use. In winter travel and especially above timberline some form of stove is almost a necessity. Wood is scarce, particularly in the more popular areas. In practice it is really best to leave the campfire for the emergency situation and plan to use the stove for cooking.

Eating Utensils

Aluminum cookware is the standard for all campers and packers. It is light and very durable. With decent care it will last many years. I have used the same mess kit for 25 years and it seems good for at least 25 more. Care should be taken to never

The old narrow-necked canteens are useful in the summer, while the wide-mouth plastic water bottles can be used year around.

boil a pot dry or to try melting snow without starter water because aluminum melts very quickly. It also should be cleaned and dried immediately after use to prevent excessive corrosion.

All sorts of pots, pans and cook kits are available. The simplest way to select the proper assortment is to determine your eating habits and carry only what you absolutely need. I should comment that with the commercial sets of silverware, a knife, fork and spoon are always included. As it is foolish to carry an ounce more than you need, and you should be carrying a jack-knife anyway, it is wise to discard the knife. If you can handle them, chopsticks are handy and can be produced readily in the field. But don't whittle them out of poison sumac or poison oak.

Speaking of letting one thing serve several purposes, a pair of pliers from your repair kit makes an excellent pot lifter and saves on fingers. For a drinking cup, either the standard stainless steel Sierra cup or a plastic cup (the ones with the measuring graduations on the sides are the best) work fine. Aluminum cups tend to get too hot and burn lips.

Water Bottles

The old narrow-necked canteens may be fine for the summer, but they are impossible to stuff with snow, which is a major source of winter water. The wide-mouth plastic water bottle seems to be the best container.

Flashlights

A good camper doesn't use a flashlight much. You set up camp and have dinner before dark. All equipment should be stowed before darkness, thereby keeping the need for light to a minimum. When you do need a light, you usually need one that you can hold in your mouth or wear on your head like a miner's headlamp, thereby freeing your hands for work. A Mallory light works especially well for a small, easily packed light. Be sure to carry both extra batteries and an extra bulb in your first-aid kit, for any light you carry.

Mandatory Equipment

Have the following in your possession *at all times,* even on the shortest trip:

    Knife—good jackknife or Swiss Army knife
    Compass
    Matches—waterproof and/or in waterproof container
    Whistle—good police-type whistle which carries a
        long distance (in very cold weather avoid metal
        whistles)
    Flashlight

This equipment is extremely important and should be *carried on your person.* Attaching a cord or lanyard to these items is frequently a good idea. It makes them easier to find if dropped in the snow.

Important Miscellaneous Equipment

Under this heading are a number of items that you also must have with you, in your pack, at all times:

    Toilet paper
    Rain gear
    Handkerchief
    Water bottle—plastic, wide-mouth
    Avalanche cord

Dry pair of gloves and socks (remember that wool
    socks can double as mittens)
Repair kit*——screwdriver, slot and phillips
     ——pliers
     ——cutting tool, ringsaw or hacksaw blade
     ——assortment of screws
     ——roll of steel wire
     ——nylon and cotton cord
     ——roll of heavy tape
     ——spare parts to ski binding
     ——spare ski tip
     ——spare ski pole basket
First-aid kit (see "Mountaineering Medicine")

Transportation

Without getting into such complex systems as dog sleds, snowmobiles, snow cats and the like, basic snow travel gets down to
hoofing it and using skis or snowshoes. The following section is
designed to give the basics and the pros and cons of the various equipment available. There will be no discussion of how to
use this equipment.

Crampons. Under mountaineering conditions of hard-packed
snow and steep-angle slopes, crampons are a necessity. Crampons are frames containing vertical steel spikes, about an inch
long, that strap to the bottoms of boots. They are used to bite
into the snow for traction when no other method is available.
They are generally used with an ice ax or other climbing aids.

Ice Ax. An ice ax is a mountaineering aid rather than a transportation device. However, for very rugged ski mountaineering it
should be considered as safety equipment. It is used to stabilize
a climber on steep slopes, as a deadman or snow anchor, or to
chop steps on icy pitches. More important, it furnishes a brake

---

*Items to be carried as group equipment. They are necessary on all trips,
but there is little point in each member of the party carrying identical items. Other items that are of a group nature and may be required on some trips include
ice saws, snow shovels, and climbing equipment. This equipment will vary from
trip to trip and should not necessarily be carried each time you go out. Be flexible and take only what you can justify, by weight and usage. No mention has
been made of toilet articles, cameras and the like. Actually, these are things that
really don't need much discussion. Bring what you need and keep it to the minimum.

Crampons — frames containing vertical steel spikes (about an inch long) that strap to the bottoms of boots — are used to bite into the snow for traction when no other method is available.

to arrest a fall on a high angle pitch of ice and snow. Should a climber fall on such a slope he should flip over onto his abdomen facing uphill. The ax is held across the chest so that a climber may dig the pick into the snow with the upper hand and shoulder, while he digs the toes of his boots into the snow. This is called self-arrest and should be practiced many times prior to using an ax on a climb.

Snowshoes. When snow is soft it does not support much weight. For convenience we'll use round numbers. Let's say we have a 200-pound hiker. The area of the sole of his boot is about 50 square inches. This means that he will exert about four pounds per square inch on the surface of the snow. This is far more weight than soft snow can support and the boot sinks into the snow. Antigravity devices are not in common use at present, so it is impossible to reduce the weight of the hiker. So, the only answer is to increase the area of his shoes. Snowshoes are devices that increase the area of the bottom of the foot, thus reducing the pounds per square inch, and thereby allowing you to walk on the snow. As they are used today they consist of a hardwood frame with rawhide stretched in a network between the frame and a harness to hold the foot. Some plastic versions are on the market, but the standard remains the wood and rawhide. Except for the leather harness the entire snowshoe is covered with a heavy coat of protective varnish. This must be redone each year to keep the shoe in good condition. Snowshoes are made in a number of designs ranging from the rounded bear paw that has an area of about 300 square inches (thereby reducing the pressure of our 200-pound man down to 0.67 pounds per square inch), to the trail model that has an area of about 600 square inches (exerts a load pressure of 0.33 pounds per square inch). The basic design types and their uses are listed below.

Bear paw—This is the shortest and widest shoe. It is for short-distance travel only, and works particularly well in heavy brush. Because of its size it can be strapped to the back of a pack and used for short treks across deep snow, a condition especially common to early spring pack trips.

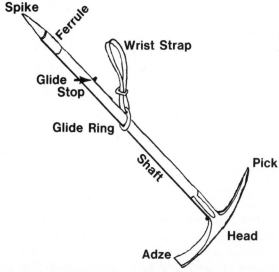

The ice ax is used to stabilize a climber on steep slopes, as a dead man or snow anchor or to chop steps on icy pitches.

If a climber begins to fall on a high angle pitch of ice and snow, he should flip onto his abdomen facing uphill, and hold his ice ax across his chest so that he may dig the pick into the snow with the upper hand and shoulder, while he digs the toes of his boots into the snow.

Green mountain bear paw—This style is a working shoe commonly used around a cabin or possibly a farmyard in winter. It is longer and heavier than the standard bear paw and is therefore unsuited for packs, but has more area for support.

Michigan—The Michigan is a compromise between trail shoes and bear paws. It is similar to the bear paw, being short and wide, but the front end is swept up like a ski and it has a tail. Unfortunately, like most compromises it doesn't do either job very well. It does work well for short trips and as a work shoe. Again, it is commonly found around farms, especially in the midwest, where it is apt to be less brushy.

Cross-country—For any extended travel over the snow, a longer narrower snowshoe is required. The cross country model has a swept up front and a long tail. The tail on these longer shoes drags in the snow behind the hiker and serves to keep the shoe pointed straight ahead. The rounded shovel helps to ride up onto the snow. As the model's name might indicate, they are excellent for long and light-pack trips.

Trail— For extended trips or ones that require heavier packs, this is the best snowshoe. It is long—about five feet from tip to tail—and has a very large upswept shovel and a long tail. The longer the snowshoe the harder it is to turn, which is a considerable disadvantage in heavy brush, but for long hauls one must sacrifice the extra weight and ease of maneuverability for support and trailing effect.

Skis

Whereas the snowshoe only moves forward to the extent of the travelers' stride, the ski adds the ability to glide forward over the snow, thereby greatly extending the length of an individual stride. There is also the added advantage of sliding forward downhill. Considerably narrower than the snowshoe, skis pose balance problems and are difficult to turn, especially when going downhill while wearing a pack.

Skis are divided into two general categories, the Alpine ski and the Nordic ski. A third category, the mountaineering ski, is actually a compromise between the other two.

Alpine Skis. These are designed exclusively for downhill travel. They are heavier and wider than Nordic skis and they employ safety bindings that lock the heel flat on the ski. The boots are high, extremely rigid and designed to give maximum support to the lower leg. Using this equipment, it is all but impossible to travel uphill; cross-country travel would be extremely fatiguing. Where use of these skis is necessary in an uphill situation, skins must be used. These will be discussed later.

Nordic Skis. For cross-country travel this is the best ski. It is far lighter, narrower and more flexible than its downhill cousin. The bottom of the ski is made of a material (wood-covered with pine tar or synthetic bases) to which wax will readily adhere. The binding is lighter and designed to hold only the toe, allowing the heel to rise off the ski. Boots are light and flexible, ranging from one that appears more like a track shoe than a ski boot, to an ankle-high version used in mountaineering. The ski is designed to glide smoothly over the snow, sticking slightly when the forward motion stops, thereby allowing the skier to kick off for another long glide. Without the heel locked down they do not turn well going downhill, but with time and some luck one can master even this obstacle.

Since cross-country skiing is of prime concern, consideration should be given to a general discussion of the various types of cross-country skis and their advantages. Like downhill or Alpine skis, the Nordic skis are highly specialized. They range from ultra-light, highly flexible racing skis to fairly heavy, rigid mountaineering skis. In their construction all Nordic skis have a few things in common besides being narrow.

Traditionally, they have been constructed of laminations of wood; usually spruce, but also birch, beech and ash. The sole of the ski is almost always made of hickory or birch — both are good rugged woods which hold wax well. The edges are often reinforced with strips of lignostone (a combination of compressed beechwood and plastic). While not equal to steel or aluminum, the lignostone edge is very hard and gives some edge bite, as well as preventing the edges of the skis from becoming badly worn.

In recent years, there have been some major breakthroughs in the construction of Nordic skis. Fiberglass and plastic-laminated skis are now often available in ski shops, However, while skis made of these materials are still well below the cost of the Alpine ski, they aren't cheap. Also, while the tips of the new skis seem nearly indestructible, they do occasionally fail under the binding. (Should this ever occur in the back country, remove the binding and move it forward on the ski, producing one short ski. While on Nordic Patrol, I have come across this problem several times and found the remedy works very well.) However, I have been told that ski manufacturers are working to correct this problem.

Another somewhat recent development is the non-wax ski bottom. A ski with this construction usually has a fish scale effect, or has longer step-like wedges cut into the bottom of the ski. This type of ski is good for beginners, but does not seem to satisfy an experienced cross-country skier. The angle of the fish scales or small steps along the bottom of the ski produces the effect of a slight drag, so these skis require slightly more energy to travel on the level or uphill. They are also very noisy, making a whirring sound as the ski glides over the snow.

Another type of waxless ski employs strips of mohair attached to the bottom of the ski. In ideal snow conditions they work well enough, but in my experience, they do not do the job in transitional snow conditions.

Racing Skis. These are the lightest and therefore the most fragile of the Nordic skis. They weigh approximately 3.5 pounds per pair, and are about two inches in width at the bindings. They are functional only on smooth terrain or in prepared tracks. They are very light, extremely flexible and very fast, but their construction makes them unacceptable for rough country.

Light Touring Skis. These are somewhat more sturdy skis designed for fast, light travel in relatively easy terrain. They work best on packed trails but can be used on unpacked surfaces. Their width averages less than three inches and they weigh about 4.5 pounds. Light touring skis do very well in low rolling country such as is found in much of the eastern United States, and make exceptionally good day touring skis. In the opinion of most tourers they are too light to stand the strain of mountain touring. However, they have been used by a few experts for rugged tours.

General Touring Skis. The work horse of the touring skis, they are go anywhere, do anything skis, weighing approximately 6.5

pounds per pair and running about three inches wide. They are light and lively enough for pleasure, yet their greater mass allows one to travel through even windpacked snow on high mountain tours. Ski mountaineers often use these skis with an aluminum or plastic edge for greater control on hardpack, crust and ice.

Mountaineering. The heaviest and stiffest of all Nordic skis, these range up to three and a half inches in width and weigh about seven pounds per pair. They are equipped with steel edges and usually run somewhat shorter than the other skis listed, depending on the desired usage — i.e., the steeper the mountain, the shorter the ski.

Alpine Skis. As a comparison, alpine skis are about three and a half to four inches wide and weigh 10 to 11 pounds per pair.

Care of Skis

The tops and edges of wooden skis should be sanded smooth so that splinters do not develop and the wood should be sealed with a good varnish. The skis may also be treated with paraffin to prevent snow from building up on the top of the ski while it is in use. If after using your skis they are covered with snow, you can prevent their ends from cracking by placing the skis, tip down, against a wall. This allows the water to run off, so the ends of the skis will not sit in a puddle of water all night. When transporting skis on a car's roof rack, place the tips toward the rear if the auto. Wind pressure from high-speed driving can snap a tip, or the vibration of the continued buffeting effect of the wind can fatigue the material. Maintaining a good pine tar base on the ski at all times is essential and will seal the bottom, preventing changes in moisture content of the wood.

Bindings

On all cross-country skis it is important that the heel be free to lift off the ski. There are two basic types of bindings in use: toe clamps and bindings that employ a cable around the heel. In all but the most rugged usage, the toe clamp is probably best. Cable bindings give better control in downhill situations and are used by ski mountaineers. At no time should the cable be locked down at the heel. This creates a bear trap type of binding and the skier is asking for a broken leg. There are a couple of bindings on the market which employ a locked-down heel with a safety release built into the cable, however, anytime a complex mechanism is used you are increasing the chance for failure.

Ski Poles

Nordic poles are somewhat longer than Alpine poles. The pole should reach directly under the arm pit when the skier is standing on a hard surface. The tips must be sharp and curved forward to avoid sticking when the poles are drawn out of the snow behind the skier. Small baskets are used by racers who are on packed snow and interested in weight. Larger baskets are favored by those who do a lot of bushwhacking in deep powder. Poles are constructed from imported cane, fiberglass and aircraft alloy tubing, the latter being the most expensive and durable. Fiberglass poles should be avoided as they shatter when they break and do not lend themselves to field repair.

Skins

Mohair skins are canvas-backed belts of mohair that are stretched under the ski in such a manner that the natural grain of the hair lies toward the back. This allows the hair to lie down as the ski slides forward, but causes it to stand up and resist backsliding. Skins are used when it is necessary for Alpine skis to be used going uphill or in some instances on mountaineering skis. They will allow a skier to move uphill beyond the ability of a wax to hold. They are heavy, awkward and tend to stretch, loosen when wet, and freeze when it gets cold, but in some cases they are the only means of travel up steep slopes.

Creepers

These are like mini crampons used under the foot on the base of the ski. They are more extensively used throughout the eastern United States, where icy conditions are common. In conditions of good old New England blue ice they are probably the only way to travel and can be strapped to the sole of boots as well as the base of skis. Similar versions are used by ice fishermen on the lakes and ponds of the northeast.

Related Reading

Equipment is changing very rapidly and it is hard to
update it in book form. The major magazines
annually review equipment in detail. For additional information see books listed under "general."

Kemsley, William Jr. and the Editors of Backpacker
Magazine, *Backpacking Equipment: A Consum-
ers Guide.* Collier' MacMillian Publishers, Lon-
don, England, 1975

6

Camping Techniques

Now for some of the fine points that can change a snow camping trip from a second-rate dinner and an uncomfortable night in a cold tent into a comfortable, enjoyable evening. Of course, in order to make such a change most of it has to come from within you. There are a few people who would be uncomfortable in the Presidential Suite of the Hilton. If you or your companion are of that ilk don't go snow camping. On the other hand, if you can take the attitude that no matter how rough things get, it's a hell of a lot better than letting your body and mind rot away in front of the boobtube, then you are on your way.

The time to start setting up your camp is before you buy the tent. Getting the equipment that is right for your needs and that you can handle well is essential.

First of all, never pick a tent which requires use of your skis or ski poles as part of its frame. This will prevent evening travel and is too restrictive.

Also, do not wait until you are in a snow camp to break out the new tent. Practice setting it up in your backyard or home-town park. Pack and unpack your pack several times, trying to maximize efficiency of weight and order. Try out your cooking techniques and all recipes at home. Trying to read the instructions when you are freezing your fanny and holding a flashlight between your teeth is not the way to go about it. Some backyard practice can make a first-time knee-knocker look like Snow Shoe Thompson — even if it is just in his own mind.

Camping Selection

The best time to look for a good campsite is before you really need it. Fumbling about in the dark trying to set up a camp in deep snow is one of the joys of winter outdoorsmanship most of us can do without. The same goes for storm conditions; high winds, heavy snow or pouring rain do not make the job any easier. In fact, a combination of any of the above can make it nearly impossible. Always plan on stopping at least two to three hours before sunset.

If night is coming on or the weather is closing in and you are still short of your objective, do not push on and risk hazardous travel or exposure to the elements. Setting up camp early while there is still plenty of light before you become tired and cold can make all the difference in the world in the enjoyment and safety of any trip. Remember also that as the sun goes down it tends to get colder quickly, and while you may be quite warm under a pack while traveling, you can get pretty chilly doing camp chores.

The single most important factor in setting up a camp is where to put it. As in everything else, safety is the first thing to think of when selecting a campsite. Avalanche chutes are not considered by most to be the smartest place to set up your happy home. Neither is close in under a cliff where items such as blocks of ice can fall from above. If you are in a wooded area, look up into the trees and check for the presence of any large dead limbs. These (with some justification) are referred to as widow makers. They can fall during the night if the wind should blow or it starts to snow. Also check around for any dead trees that could topple. Check for the presence of ice balls formed on tree limbs. These are produced by melted snow refreezing to form balls of ice which cling to smaller branches. If one of these breaks loose from the upper branches of a tree, it could rip through your tent, or raise a sizeable lump on someone's head. Also, if you are in the high country make sure there are no large rocks lying on top of the snow.

Camping on the top of a ridge may prevent things from falling on you all night. However, it may become a bit too airy for comfort if a high wind comes up. A narrow, protected bench on a mountainside may be safe when you are working with your boots on and the snow is soft from the day's sun. At night, should you get up to answer a call of nature, you may not have any traction and find yourself tumbling down a mountainside. This may sound humorous but it has proved fatal. Avoiding these and other hazards such as setting your tent astride the entrance to a hibernating grizzly bear's den, you may then consider the comfort and convenience of a good campsite.

Remember, cold air is heavier than warm air and it settles. At night this cold air will settle into places like pothole valleys, canyon bottoms or almost any depression. Also avoid areas that become natural funnels for the wind whistling down from high peaks. Camping near a stream may be convenient, but consider the dampness that will accompany the evening chill. A warm bench on a gentle hillside among some trees or near some other natural windbreak is a good area to pick. Keep in mind that the uphill flow of air in the daytime will change to a downhill flow at night. Camp on the downhill side of a windbreak or on the lee side of the prevailing wind.

In level country seek a good windbreak in a brush pile, a stand of trees, or a cluster of rocks. Of course, try to determine which way the wind will be blowing; being on the windward side of a windbreak isn't much help. Camping under trees that are heavily laden with snow, while not necessarily dangerous, can give you quite a shower if the trees start to unload. About a hundred yards back from any open water is also a good rule to follow, both to avoid the chill and any pollution of the water.

Setting Up Camp

In this discussion we are going to talk about tent camping only. Alternative shelters such as snow caves are covered under "Survival," more for convenience than any implied warning against their use.

Once the decision has been made to place a camp in a given location, the site must be prepared. If you can find a clear, dry area, so much the better. If not, the snow should undergo some preparation. Before you remove your skis or snowshoes, tramp the snow down to give a firm platform to work on. Using your skis, pack down the snow by sidestepping, first in one direction and then *at right angles*. A little extra comfort may be gained if, when you are stomping around to pack the snow down, you remember to stomp in a hip hole. This is a slight indentation about the size and shape of your pelvis. If you lie absolutely flat on hard-packed snow, with only a ⅜-inch foam pad under you, you may wake during the night with a very sore area on the bonier sections of the pelvis. After the snow is packed firmly, you may remove the boards and continue packing with your boots. It also helps to pack in a couple of trails with your skis to such vital areas as the water supply and the toilet. This need not be a major project, but at night it helps if you have a track in the snow to follow.

Once a solid platform has been packed in the snow, there is a little trick to which direction the tent should face. If a tent is set up so that it faces into the wind and a small opening is left in the front, the wind will blow into the tent and fill it like a balloon. Once filled, not much more wind will enter and the air inside will become warm and stay in the tent. If you set the tent sideways to the wind, the sides of the tent will flap all night long, acting like a bellows. Not only is this noisy, but it will pump all the warm air out of the tent and you will freeze.

When setting up a tent in the snow, you will find there are a few things you didn't consider during your warm-weather practice sessions. First, the temperature. Nylon is an unbelievably cold item to handle in winter. As a result, it is a good idea to wear lightweight gloves that will allow you the manual dexterity but which will prevent frostbite. Also, don't just toss the tent out and go tromping about carelessly in the snow. Use deliberate movements; by so doing you avoid kicking snow into the tent. Remember that a tent is supposed to be a warm dry shelter.

The usual stakes furnished with a backpack tent are aluminum pegs. But these do not hold in the snow, so save the weight and leave them at home. As an alternative, purchase long angular aluminum or high-impact plastic stakes. Either of these hold reasonably well if stomped into the snow and packed in correctly. A device which works far better, however, is a "dead man." This consists of a bag filled with snow or a large rock you can tie your line to. The bag or rock is then buried and packed into the surrounding snow. This will do a better job than just a peg driven into the snow. Another method is to obtain a long stick and dig a slit trench perpendicular to the tent. Lay the stick into the trench, attach lines and bury it. This is another application of the "dead man" principal.

If you must camp in an exposed location subject to high winds, double lash your tent. Use extra lines and keep the tent walls as tight as possible. On high mountain peaks, winter winds of 100 mph are not uncommon. Tents blown from their lashings and torn apart by high winds are a frequent cause of climbing accidents.

As soon as the tent is set up and any snow that has accidently been kicked inside is removed, lay your foam pad down and fluff out your sleeping bag. This should be done as soon as possible to allow time for your bag to loft before you crawl in. This will insure maximum warmth from the bag. If the day is warm and sunny and you have already spent one night in your sleeping bag, it is a good idea to open your bag and hang it over a dry tree or even your tent. This allows the bag to air out and dry before you use it again.

Once the tent is up, getting in a good supply of water and firewood is the next order of business. In winter, these normally simple chores can present some problems.

First, you should consider whether or not you are going to build a fire. In national parks, the rangers are doing everything in their power to discourage the practice. In other regions that may receive heavy usage, campfires probably should be avoided for ecological reasons. Firewood has become scarce and the ashes of winter fires can leave a grand mess after the snow has melted. If you are in an area where a fire may be suitable, try to keep it as small as possible. Use the philosophy of the Indians: Build a small fire and sit close. You will be just as warm as you would be building a monstrous fire and then standing several yards away. As a rule, you should avoid fires and carry a stove whenever possible.

Dry wood can be found even in wet weather, if you gather the dead branches that remain on the lower parts of older trees. This is called squaw wood and is very hard and dry. Even when it has been raining, this type of dead wood will not soak up water and will burn, if the surface can be dried a bit. Always build your fires well away from your tent. Sparks or the heat of a campfire can spell disaster for a tent.

Before building a fire in the snow, a base of larger logs or flat stones should be laid in the fire pit. If this is not done, the fire will melt the snow beneath it, all the way down to the bare ground. In areas where 6 to 10 feet of snow is common, this can leave the camper sitting a chilly distance from his fire.

When you are building your fire be sure to check for snow on any overhanging branches. Any rising heat will melt the snow enough to cause it to fall into your fire. It is also a good idea to build a wind screen. This can be done with a snow wall or a more elaborate device of rocks or other material. Should you use anything other than snow, put it back where you found it when you break camp. Not only will the windbreak prevent your fire from being blown out, it acts as a heat reflector. This will

If you are in an area where a fire may be suitable, try to keep it as small as possible.

greatly increase the amount of heat you receive from even a small fire. Remember, however, that rocks you use in fire are scarred and remain so for hundreds of years.

Before building the fire, gather an adequate supply of wood and lay the fire carefully. Trying to run after more wood while getting a fire going can turn a campsite into a Keystone Cops production. Start with small twigs or cut shavings off larger sticks. Build up to larger and larger sticks, being sure to pile them loosely to allow good air draft.

There are several fire-starter compounds on the market that will help in starting a winter campfire. Or if you are a do-it-yourselfer, you may produce a good fire starter with a little candle wax and some toilet paper. Use a bright orange or yellow paper that will show up if dropped into the snow. Lay the paper out in a pan in layers. Lay out the whole roll in about a two-foot strip. Pour melted paraffin over the paper, allowing it to be soaked up. The paper is then pressed into a firm sheet and allowed to harden and dry. Cut into strips, it makes a good waterproof fire starter.

A warm bench on a gentle hillside near some form of natural windbreak is a good campsite to pick.

Remember to leave your campsite just as it was when you arrived.

Matches may also be dipped in paraffin to waterproof them. But better than matches are the small disposable lighters which are quite dependable and give many lights. However, some of these lighters leak at high altitudes, so be careful where you carry them.

If the weather is bad you can use a stove in a tent that has a cook hole sewn in the bottom. Frequently check the tent walls for overheating and avoid getting your sleeping bag or other equipment near the stove. If you use a stove outside, either dig a small pit or build a windbreak around the stove. In high wind, the windbreak for either a fire or a cook stove may need to be four feet high, so do not worry about overbuilding.

A word of caution on wind breaks: If you are using a stove with a canister of compressed gas, do not completely enclose the stove and canister. The heat can build up in the rock enclosure to a point where the can of gas will explode. Recently, one person was blinded and several were injured in such an accident.

If there is no free source of water available, you must melt snow. If there is free water around, check it out just as carefully as you would in the summer. Swamp water does not taste any better because it's cold, and you can get just as sick drinking bad cold water as you can drinking bad warm water.

If not handled properly, melting snow can be an interesting experience. Snow has a fairly low water content, especially in ranges like the Rockies. A pot full of snow placed over a hot flame will cause the water to evaporate as fast as it melts and leave the pot dry. A dry aluminum pot takes little time to melt. For this reason, a little starter water should be placed in the bottom of the pot. If you have forgotten to leave a little water in the wide-mouth water bottle, then start your melting *very slowly*, over a low flame, until the bottom of the pot is covered with water. A good point to remember is that while snow has a low water content for a given volume, ice will yield a 90 percent return on the melted volume. So when possible, melt ice, not snow. Other sources of water are discussed in the chapter on survival.

A word about taste. Melted snow is like distilled water—completely tasteless and bland. It does, however, acquire taste very readily-possibly an unpleasant taste, if you are not careful. Snow gathered from pine bows or ice formed where snow on trees melts and refreezes will often have the bitter taste of the bark or pine needles. Also, icicles hanging from rocks may contain a sizable amount of minerals — often even becoming discolored. Other sources of unpleasant taste are grease from your cooking pot and smoke from a wood fire. Any of these things when mixed with the tasteless melted snow can produce a most undesirable potion.

Food

Napoleon once said an army travels on its stomach. Well, that statement is doubly true when applied to winter mountaineering situations. The body's only energy source is the food you eat. If you have had an improper intake of food you will become cold many times faster and will not be able to perform the tasks required of you. Cross-country skiing and winter mountaineering are not places to practice dieting.

Overeating at the wrong time, however, can leave food lumped in an undigested mass in your stomach. Eating a large meal just prior to heavy exercise creates a situation in which the

Setting up camp in the snow takes a little more planning than setting up camp on dry ground.

food is deposited in the stomach, but the exercise prevents it from being digested. Heavy exercise causes blood circulation to be shifted from the digestive tract to the skeletal muscles and shuts down the muscular action of the stomach. When the food hits the stomach, the stomach lining secretes hydrochloric acid to help break down the food. If digestion is stopped at that point, the food is in a large lump at the bottom of the stomach, which is filled with acid.

As a result, you have one heck of a case of heartburn as well as a bloated feeling in your stomach. If you should get into this situation, about the only good relief is to sit down and rest for awhile and let your meal digest before moving on. Usually this will take about an hour.

Different types of food are broken down and react differently in the body. Therefore, you should understand a few facts about the basic food groups and how they react within the body. The three basic food groups are *carbohydrates, proteins and fats.*

Carbohydrates. Carbohydrates are foods whose basic elements are carbon, hydrogen and oxygen; hence the name. They make up the sugars and starches. Practically applied to foods, they include sugars, grain products, most vegetables and fruits. Carbohydrates are mostly bland (except in the case of citrus fruits), easy to digest and supply the fastest source of energy to the body. They are also unlikely to contribute to altitude sickness (see "Mountaineering Medicine"). Their shortcoming lies in the fact that they are burned off fairly quickly and you must keep ingesting more at regular intervals to maintain your energy level.

Proteins. In addition to containing the basic elements of the carbohydrate group, proteins also contain nitrogen compounds and frequently sulfur compounds. These compounds are in complex formations known as amino acids. Unlike carbohydrates, which undergo a substantial part of their digestion in the stomach, proteins do not really start to be digested until they reach the small intestine. There they require an additional step before they can be absorbed by the body and used as an energy source. For this reason the energy derived from eating proteins takes longer to reach the muscles, but it also lasts longer. Pound for pound, the energy supplied by either proteins or carbohydrates is equal. The principal difference is in the time factor. In persons subject to altitude sickness, proteins tend to make them more upset than do carbohydrates.

Fats. Fats chemically consist of the same elements as the carbohydrates, but are held together in far more complex compounds, glycerine and fatty acids. Fats produce more energy: nine calories per gram as opposed to four calories per gram for proteins and carbohydrates. Even though they are an exceptional source of energy for the body, they are very hard to digest and tend to cause nausea and stomach upset. For this reason foods high in fat like salami should be treated with great caution. Also, as with proteins, fats take a long time to break down and are not a quick source of energy.

Everyone has his own peculiarities with regard to his eating habits and the manner in which he digests food. It is well to consider that high altitude and heavy exercise will increase tenfold any problems you may otherwise encounter. Stay on the safe side and watch your eating habits. An upset stomach can ruin a trip.

Breakfast. Assuming you will be traveling, hence exercising heavily shortly after breakfast, you will want to eat a light, quickly digested meal. This indicates a high carbohydrate meal. The good old bacon and eggs breakfast cooked over a wood fire may seem very romantic and is fine if you are going to be staying around camp. But it's hell to travel on. The fat and protein-from bacon will form a greasy lump in your stomach and leave you with a feeling of nausea that will last until lunch. This is important to remember especially if you are driving up to your favorite area and stop at a restaurant for breakfast. It's a temptation to see a day of hard outdoor exercise coming up and hit the ham and eggs. You'll be far better off with an order of pancakes or French toast with plenty of syrup. Hot oatmeal is another excellent breakfast. Fruits, especially the less acid ones, go down well and do not tend to upset the stomach. If you normally do not have digestion problems, some protein can be taken to give you a little staying power, but should be kept to a minimum.

Along with breakfast, it is wise to take a salt tablet or two. At high altitude it is easy to sweat a great deal without realizing it; loss of body salt is a cause of muscle cramps.

Trail Snacks. To keep up your energy and heat level it is a good idea to stop frequently and have small trail snacks. These should be almost exclusively carbohydrates. In fact, keeping a piece of hard candy in your cheek is a fairly good idea. One point to remember in connection with candy is that chocolate bars contain a lot of fat. They get very brittle when cold and melt when warm. But what is important is that they are very hard to digest. Leave the Hershey bars at home and instead bring hard candy. It stay at the same consistency hot or cold and it is almost pure sugar, thereby making it easy to digest. Honey is an excellent, but sometimes messy, trail snack. Lemon and honey drops or malted milk tablets are among the better trail snacks; while raisins, other dried fruits and granola also work very well. And remember to take frequent sips of water.

Lunch. At lunch time you will generally be stopping for a short break and not quickly jumping back to hard work. It is therefore a chance to take in a little protein or fat with the cabohydrates. But you should still keep it on the starchy side. If you are just out for the day, a good suggestion is a sandwich made out of peanut butter and honey—very good on whole wheat bread. The peanut butter contains a lot of protein and oil (fat) and is a

When setting up camp, use deliberate movements to avoid kicking snow into the tent.

lasting energy source that is fairly easy to digest. The bread and honey also provide a quick source of energy. Cheeses and French bread also work great, as well as any of the grain products and dried fruits.

Drink water regularly and in small amounts to prevent dehydration from too much sweating. Also Tang and other powdered fruit drinks are good and are easily mixed for any meal. Hot tea and honey is good, too.

Dinner. This is the meal where the fats and protein belong. With camp set up and the day's activity behind you, it is a time when you can more easily digest a larger meal. The slower breakdown of the protein will keep the body warm through the night and will stave off early morning hunger. On short weekend ovenighters there is no reason why fresh food cannot be carried. The weather is cold enough to prevent meat from spoiling. The outdoorsman need only be careful to carry it in a leak-proof container to prevent the juice from leaking all over your pack.

Another trick is to bring along some of the frozen foods available in plastic cooking pouches. Using these, dinner can be prepared by bringing a pot of water to boil, putting in a pouch of wild rice and one of your favorite vegetables, and boiling them for the prescribed time. The pot can then be set aside while you cook the meat, bringing it back to a boil again to reheat the food when the meat is done. The water in the pot which cooked the plastic pouches then can be used for tea or coffee. With a little shifting back and forth you can prepare such a meal over a one-burner stove and have it piping hot in the middle of a blizzard.

On longer or more difficult trips, the prepared freeze-dried dinners are an excellent choice. Some of these tend to be a little heavy on the carbohydrates, so exercise care in your selection. A point to remember in going the freeze-dried route is that for some people this type of food is a bit constipating, so some dried fruit brought along for dessert is a good idea. Otherwise, some of the freeze-dried puddings are excellent and make a good topping for the evening meal.

A good instant hot drink that will give plenty of energy and tastes exceptionally good can be made up at home in powdered form. The recipe is as follows.

    1 8-oz. jar of orange Tang
    1 envelope instant lemonade
    1 cup instant tea mix
    ¼ teaspoon ground cloves
    1 teaspoon cinnamon

Mix these together in the dry state and store until needed. In the field carry a small plastic bag of the mix and brew it as you would a tea. It has a very warming effect and contains a fair amount of sugar for instant energy.

In general, before you try any food in the back country try it out at home. There is no point in getting out in the back country and breaking open a freeze-dried dinner or other prepared meal and finding that you can't stand it. There is no supermarket down the street to obtain a replacement and you would be stuck eating it. The whole point is that you are out there to enjoy yourself and part of that is eating things you like.

Furthermore, you might try checking out the local supermarket for trail foods. There are many easily prepared, so-called instant dinners available, and often taste better and cost less than those in the mountain shop. Some of the stuff in the sporting goods store is very expensive. A health food store or the health food counter in the supermarket is a good source of dried cereals and fruits, as well as some of the better honey drops and other natural candies.

Regarding vitamins and minerals, missing a couple of days is not going to hurt you one bit. Unless your system is very finely balanced and you must have them for short trips, it is just so much inconvenience and you can get by without them. The dietary suggestions made in this chapter do not follow a good overall eating program. They are made for optimum results under certain circumstances and would likely constitute an unbalanced diet if taken on a prolonged basis. But unless you are going on an extended expedition, you will be unlikely to suffer any malnutrition from eating too many carbohydrates and you may well prevent a case of upset stomach or mountain sickness.

Protecting Your Food Supplies

In some regions extra care should be exercised in storing food even in the middle of the winter. Food-poaching animals have ruined many a trip, especially in the national parks where they have no fear of man. *Never sleep with food in your tent or sleeping bag.* The only time this rule can be broken would be in true mountaineering situations when your camp is situated in such a high, remote place no animal in his right mind would ever venture near it. In less remote areas, however, many persons have been hurt or killed by bears because they slept with food.

Get the food out of the sleeping area; it is best stored in a stuff bag (not your pack) hung about 15 feet from the ground. Bears are great tree climbers, so the food bag must also be hung well away from the reach of a tree-climbing bear. This can be done by stretching a line between two trees and then running the food bag up a second line tossed over the first. The food should be at least 15 feet from the nearest tree.

If bears are no problem, mice, raccoons, or porcupines certainly can be. A mouse hole chewed in the side of a good pack is a maddening sight.

If your camp is raided by a bear, they are unlikely to attack unless provoked. Do not attack them or put yourself between them and the food they are after. If you have taken proper care of the food they will be unable to get it and will give up and leave. If they do get your food you are not going to be able to get it back and may just get yourself hurt in the attempt.

Camping Courtesy

In addition to storing the food so as not to attract animals into camp, keep a clean camp. Wash your dishes as soon as any meal is completed, but never wash in a stream or lake. All you will do is leave food residue lying on the bottom of the stream and soap scum in the water. Wilderness water supplies are fragile and can be polluted easily. Do your washing by gathering water in a pot and washing it well away from the stream or pond. Dispose of dishwater by tossing it out over as large an area as possible, well away from the stream. Brillo pads are excellent pot washers for back country use. They fit into a plastic bag or a soap dish and can be used for a number of meals. Always take them with you when you leave the camp site.

If you have any garbage, store it in the same manner as you do you food until you can pack it out with you. *Do not bury rubbish in the snow.* Clean up and store rubbish as it is produced or it might accidently be covered with snow and forgotten. When the snow melts a fine mess is left for the summer camper. Pack out everything you bring in. Such things as orange peels last a very long time if left lying around. Many people get the idea that if it's organic it will rot or the animals will eat it and no one will notice. What really happens is that it freezes in the snow and lies around on the ground half the summer. No one wants his favorite park or wilderness area turned into a trash dump. So take care of your own mess and clean up that of anyone else who might have left things thrown about.

The camp toilet can present similar troubles in the winter. The freezing effect applies to human waste as well as to garbage. The toilet must be located well away from summer use areas and water supplies. Burn toilet paper after use. If just tucked under the snow, it will not decompose, and as the snow melts will be found draped from a bush. This is not the most appealing welcome to the summertime visitor. Of course if you can find a bare area, bury human waste whenever possible.

Other Tips

Once the evening meal is done and the camp is cleaned up there are a few tricks to making the night pass a little smoother. Packs are bulky items to sleep with in a tent. They are best protected by carrying a large trash bag and sliding it down over the pack at night. This works well summer or winter, as even the most water-resistant pack can suffer from some leakage in wet weather.

Trash bags are a handy item to have along anyway, as they can serve as an emergency poncho by slitting a head hole in the bottom and wearing them upside down. In first-aid situations they can serve as sleeping bag covers. In fact, they even work well as trash bags.

Pack your bag by using a number of clear bags for any group of items: This will keep things together and dry. In this manner underclothes and socks can be packed in a bag and taken into the tent. You will then not have to poke through a pile of clothes to find a single sock the next morning. Once changed, the same bag doubles as a laundry bag.

Small items like jackknives, match cases, can openers and the like should be tied together by a small, colored cord. Then if they are dropped into the snow they can be retrieved more easily. It works on the same principal as an avalanche cord. In this respect vital items like a compass and whistle should be worn on a lanyard around your neck, just to make sure they do not disappear. Also try and discourage borrowing around the camp. Keep your own personal items and then if you lose something you have only yourself to blame.

Cold temperatures slow down all chemical reactions. As a result flashlight batteries may appear to go dead very quickly on cold nights. For this reason, carrying your flashlight in your inside pocket except when in use will give you better light than leaving it in a pack. Also, sticking it down inside the sleeping bag at night is quite helpful.

Along the same lines, you might give some thought to the batteries in the light meter of your camera. In very cold weather such meters can show incorrect readings and incorrectly expose film.

Another problem encountered in a tent on a cold night is the accumulation of frost on the inside of the tent. As a person sleeps he perspires and exhales a great deal of moisture in his breath. This loss amounts to about a quart of water each night. With two people in the average mountain tent this adds up to a half a gallon of water. The warm moist air so produced hits the cold wall of the tent and condenses, freezing at once into a layer of frost. With any movement of the tent wall this can flake off, producing a small snowstorm inside the tent.

In very cold climates a frost liner may be necessary for your tent. This is a second layer of fabric the same shape as the tent but suspended inside the regular tent. The liner is made from an absorbent cotton which will soak up the water before it freezes, thereby trapping the ice crystals and preventing the snow shower. It acts as a double wall for the tent, greatly increasing its interior warmth, In the morning, simply unfasten the frost liner and take it outside and beat it like a carpet to get rid of the frost. Otherwise the only way to get the frost out of the tent is to let the sun warm it during the day and allow plenty of ventilation.

If the weather is bad, wiping down the walls of the tent with a soft dry cloth helps to some degree. With the possibility of snow being kicked into the tent and the formation of frost on the inside, clothes left loose inside the tent may be quite damp in the morning. Dry clothes should be stored in the sleeping bag cover or a plastic bag. Clothes that are only slightly damp can be tucked down in the foot of the sleeping bag and dried to some extent that way. Wet clothes present quite a problem but they can be dried if suspended from a clothesline strung across the top of the tent while a small stove is kept burning. This is not the best procedure and should be used only in times of emergency.

Small items like glasses can be tucked inside the boots. This will keep them from being lost .and you will certainly find them when you put the boots on in the morning. Bringing a water bottle into the tent, making sure the top is screwed on tightly, is also a good idea. It usually prevents the water from freezing and will give you a drink if you should wake up dry in the middle of the night.

In the morning when you break camp, put everything back just as it was when you arrived. If you have moved rocks, scatter them about as they were. The same goes for any stacks or poles you may have put up. Leave the campsite with only your tracks to show that anyone was there.

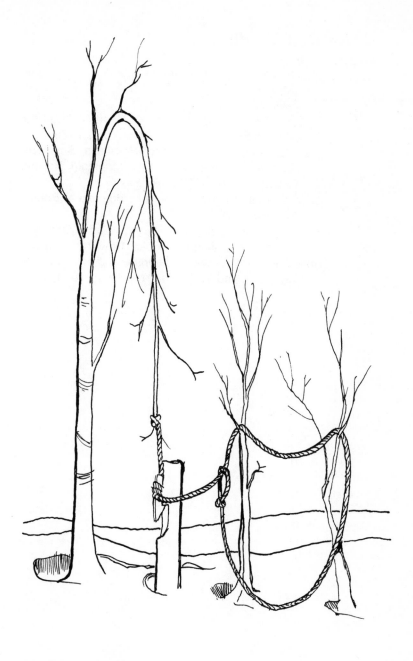

A snare can be useful in capturing small game for food.

Related Reading

Adirondack Mountain Club, Inc. *Winter Hiking and Camping.* Adirondack Mountain Club, Inc., Glen Falls, NY

Bridge, *The Complete Snow Campers' Guide.* Charles Scribner's Sons, New York, 1973

Fear, Eugene, *Outdoor Living; Problems, Solutions, Guidelines.* Tacoma Unit of Mountain Rescue Council, Tacoma WA, 1970

Graves, Richard H. *Bushcraft.* Schocken Books, New York, 1972.

Brower, David, edit. *The Sierra Club Wilderness Handbook.* Ballantine Books, New York, 1971

Rossit, Edward A. *Snow Camping and Mountaineering.* Funk and Wagnalls, New York, 1974

7

Mountaineering Medicine

This section provides information on specialized problems that are encountered in cold climates or at high altitude. It should not be considered a first-aid course.

It is imperative that each back country traveler maintain a current first-aid card.

In back country travel or under the stress of high altitude, normal first-aid procedures may not be adequate. There is no ambulance or rescue squad just a phone call away. You may be alone, and help could be miles or days away. The margin for error becomes much smaller and the necessity of just keeping an injured person alive for several days may arise. If these thoughts seem a little scary, they should! Even the best stocked first-aid pouch can be slim pickings in a real emergency.

Before you venture out, it is wise to learn all you can about the normal body functions. Watch yourself and your companions for any changes in normal patterns. When traveling, occasionally ask how your companions feel and do not hesitate to speak up about any of your own complaints. At high altitude even a minor upset stomach can be a horrible experience. Stop and treat any small problem at once before it becomes a major one.

Basic Travel Rules

If you do not feel well, stay at home.

Obtain the correct count of your group and get each member's name.

Check over the first-aid supplies of the group.

There is little point in massive duplication of equipment, so know who has what.

The leader and tail must be informed of any physical problems of any party member. They should also know the usage of all medication carried on the trip.

In the back country go to extremes to avoid accidnets.

Back Country Emergency Procedure

Analyze the sitution, making the best diagnosis possible.

Administer emergency first aid.

Gather all facts and write them down.

Injured:
—Degree of injury.
—Present condition.
—Name and address.

Location:
—Exactly where victims are located.
—Special equipment required.
—Easiest evacuation route.
—Time required for evacuation.

Evacuate victim as soon as possible or establish a shelter and send for help. Be sure the persons going for help carry a copy of the information listed above.

Sunburn

At high altitude, air is less dense and a whole lot cleaner. Therefore, it does not filter the sun's ultraviolet rays as well as does the stuff most of us are used to living in. This greatly increases the burning effects and drastically cuts the exposure time required to become sunburned. Add to this the reflected rays from all of that beautiful snow and you are apt to get a burn where you have never been burned before; under the chin or ears or how about inside your nose or the roof of your mouth, if you are panting away, going up a steep hill. Toss in the drying effect of wind and low humidity and it's time to really smear on the old suntan lotion and lip ice. No matter how nice the weather may be, it's a good place to keep your clothes on. A loosely worn white shirt is cool and will reflect the sun's rays. If you go very high or are exposed for long periods, the white or zinc oxide creams, such as glacier cream, may be necessary.

Snow Blindness

In addition to burning the skin and mucous membranes, those ultraviolet rays can cook your eyes. Always, even on overcast days, wear protective glasses or goggles because snow blindness can occur in as little time as a half hour. If you lose your glasses, replace them with a band of cloth with slits cut in it (Eskimo sunglasses). Also, blacken the rims of the eyes and wear a visored cap. Sunburned eyes start with a burning of the surface of the eye (cornea and conjuctiva), but may progress to affect the retina or nerve bed at the rear of the eye. During the period of exposure, there may be no sensation other than brightness to warn the victim. Symptoms may be delayed for 8 to 12 hours before becoming apparent. The eyes feel dry, as though there is sand in them, and moving or blinking becomes extremely painful. Exposure to light may cause pain. Eyelids become swollen and red and there is excessive tearing. Severe cases may last several days but will heal spontaneously. The victim must not rub his eyes. Some relief may be obtained from cold compresses and a darkened environment. Ophalmic ointment containing cortisone gives relief from the pain and shortens the course of the condition.

Muscle Cramps

Common to all is the good old charlie horse. When an overworked muscle builds up too much lactic acid or is lacking in necessary body salt, it contracts and stays that way. The offending muscle is not too hard to find, primarily because of the pain it's causing. A little probing around in the area should yield a muscle that feels hard and tight. Disregarding the victim's pleas for mercy, administer a good firm massage with particular attention to stretching along the muscle until you locate a single very tender spot (the trigger point). Apply firm thumb pressure over this point a few minutes until it becomes numb, then go back to the massage.

To prevent cramps, condition properly before the season. Before traveling, loosen and stretch out muscles stiffened by sleep or long auto rides. In addition, take salt tablets because you can sweat a lot while cross-country skiing. If you are especially prone to cramps, try taking calcium tablets on a daily basis (bone meal tablets work best). A good dosage is about 750 mg per day. Calcium is necessary in the blood to prevent muscle cramps and if you tend to have this trouble, it may be the answer. If this does not solve the problem, consult your physician.

Hypothermia (Exposure)

This is nature's great silent killer that claims more victims than any other cause. Simply stated, hypothermia is the insidious loss of heat from the body. How many times have you read in the newspapers of someone becoming lost and dying from exposure? What they are talking about is hypothermia. The condition can creep in and strike down a victim while his companions march along, totally unaware of the situation until it is too late. The inner core temperature of the victim's body will have dropped to a degree where normal metabolism breaks down. Death will result, unless the heat loss is discovered and reversed.

To understand hypothermia, we must consider how the body produces and conserves its heat and how it may be lost by those venturing out in cold, wet or windy weather. Food is converted by the body into heat and energy. Carbohydrates (sugars and starches) metabolize very quickly and are a fast source of heat and ernergy. Proteins are equally good but require a longer time to break down. Fats, pound for pound, produce twice the heat of either protein or carbohydrates, but for some are harder to digest. Muscular activity is a second source of heat. Stop moving and you cool down, start climbing a steep hill and you warm up fast. Shivering is an example of the body's attempt to use muscular activity to warm itself. Outside sources of heat are the sun, fires and hot foods. Once the body has produced heat it tries to conserve it. When the body cools, surface blood vessels contract; this cools the extremities but keeps the warmer blood near the vital core. The body is insulated with a layer of fat just below the skin. Because women have an extra thickness of this tissue, they can withstand cold slightly better than men can.

Just as the body produces and stores heat, it also continually loses it. *Freezing temperatures are not necessary for this heat loss to occur.* Heat is lost through respiration; you breathe in cold air, heat it up and exhale warm air. You lose heat by perspiration and its subsequent evaporation from the skin. The body is constantly trying to warm the air around it or any water that may collect on it. If this air or moisture moves from the body, it takes some of the body's heat with it. Like any other warm object, the body will radiate heat from any uncovered portion. Contact with cold objects, getting wet or exposure to wind, can reduce or destroy the protective warming effect of clothing. Again, remember that wool is the one fabric which retains some of its warming qualities when wet.

Particular attention should be given to protecting body areas where blood vessels lie close to the skin. The scalp has an extremely rich vascular bed; it is relatively thin and stretched over bone; and with few exceptions, is not protected by much fat. An uncovered head can radiate up to 30 percent of the body heat. The neck and throat also are areas where large blood vessels lie near the skin and are often left unprotected. The wrists, too, must be considered as potential heat loss sources. A further note of caution: The practice of eating snow places the cold snow directly in contact with the rich vascular beds of the mouth and will certainly help cool the body.

Hypothermia occurs any time the cooling effects exceed the production of heat in the body. Remember, people have died from hypothermia in 50-degree weather. A hiker who becomes exhausted in cold, damp weather will move slower and slower, producing less and less heat from muscular activity. If he has not eaten well, his body may not be producing enough heat to replace his heat losses. Add to this the psychological factors of the victim's senses becoming slowly dulled and the hiker is in grave trouble. The symptoms usually occur insidiously and can proceed to a danger point before recognized.

The following table gives some signs to watch for:

BODY TEMPERATURE	SYMPTOMS
99 to 96	Uncontrolled shivering, victim looks cold. Will be quiet, not speaking much.
92 to 91	Shivering more violent, coordination deteriorates, pace slows, begins to stumble, thinking slowed, unable to speak.
87 to 86	Shivering ceases, muscles become stiff, unable to walk.

82 to 81   Muscles become rigid, pulse and respiration
                      slowed.

80 or less   Unconsciousness and death.

Treatment. Once hypothermia has begun, the body loses its
ability to rewarm itself. Stopping the further loss of heat is insuf-
ficient. *External sources of heat must be applied to the body.*
Treatment consists of three steps:

Prevent further heat loss.
Warm the body, using external heat sources.
Administer foods to supply fuel for the body.

On the trail, this may amount to setting as a shelter and getting
the victim inside. Remove all wet clothing, undress him and put
him in a sleeping bag. Get undressed yourself and crawl in with
him. Massage his body, work the muscles to get the blood moving. Talk to him, keep him awake and be encouraging. Give him
warm liquid if he is conscious. (*Never try to administer fluids to
an unconscious person.)* Give him sugar or candy — even an
unconscious person can absorb a little sugar, if it is placed under his lower lip. Build a fire if possible. *Do anything to get him
warm.*

Frostbite

Where hypothermia is a cooling of the body core, frostbite involves damage to extremities caused by loss of circulation and
localized freezing. When this affects only the skin, it is called
superficial frostbite. When it involves deep tissue muscle, tendon
and bone it is called *deep frostbite.* The distinction is important
because the treatments for the two conditions differ. In the case
of frostbitten tissue, ice crystals develop between the cells, and
as the ice crystals increase in size water is withdrawn from the
cells. Biochemical changes occur within the cells, which can
lead to their death. There is also a critical temperature, about
27° F, at which these changes become irreversible and permanent tissue damage results. The progressive degrees of frostbite
may be described as follows:

Initial biting cold, leading to numbness. Some red-
    ness and puffiness appears.
Tissue swells more, skin turns violet. If unchecked,
    this leads to a hard woody feeling and the skin
    becomes yellowish white.

Skin becomes puffed and shiny, blisters appear, coloration may be rose or violet.

Blisters break, tissue scars and peels away. Stopped at this point, six months may show only partial healing and there will be some permanent damage.

Blisters dry, turn black and slough off. Infection or gangrene may set in. Amputation or skin grafts are usually necessary.

Prevention is again the name of the game. Keep extremities warm and do not restrict circulation with tight-fitting boots or clothing. Stop and warm body part that is getting too cold and avoid handling metal equipment without gloves.

If forced to spend a night out on a bivouac, there are a few additional precautions. Remove all glasses, watches, earrings and rings. If climbing and using crampons, they also should be removed. Any of these items will conduct heat from the body.

In addition arms can be drawn inside the jacket with the sleeves turned inside out and crossed inside the back of the jacket for additional warmth. All tight clothing should be loosened to prevent constriction of blood flow. This is especially true of boots. Exposure of any portion of the body should be reduced to an absolute minimum.

Treatment of Superficial Frostbite. As mentioned previously, superficial frostbite is a blanching of the skin over the affected area, accompanied by a loss of sensation. It can be treated on the spot by rapid rewarming, using any gentle means available. Stick your cold fingers under your armpit, your cold toes inside a companion's clothes against his skin or cover your cold nose with a warm hand. Then protect that body part from further cold. Thawing is accompanied by a tingling or burning sensation and the skin may become quite red. Blisters may appear later, but should never be broken. *Never rub frostbitten tissue*; this only leads to further tissue damage.

Treatment of Deep Frostbite. This involves a great deal of treatment and should *never* be attempted on the trail. Once the treatment is started, the victim will become completely disabled. A person can walk for days on frozen feet and not do much further damage to them, but once rewarmed, he will be in severe pain and unable to walk. Once the patient has reached a medical facility or, in some cases, a well-equipped base camp from which he may be transported, treatment consists of *rapid rewarming in hot water*, between 108° and 112°F. Rewarming will take from 20 to 30 minutes. Treatment in this matter causes extreme pain. However, it results in far less tissue damage than the old method of slower rewarming. Medication for relieving pain must be used. After the part is rewarmed, it is treated the same as an open wound or severe burn.

Trench Foot

This condition became prevalent during World War I, when thousands of troops stood in cold, mud-filled trenches for days at a time. It is the breakdown of the skin on the feet due to prolonged exposure to cold, wet conditions. Similar conditions have been observed in cross-country skiers who got their feet wet and failed to dry their socks; continuing to ski for several days with cold wet socks can leave the feet in very bad condition. The skin becomes white and dead in appearance, and may blister and slough off. The sores so produced can last for weeks and require much treatment. An extra pair of warm dry socks is the best prevention and should always be carried in your pack. If your feet get wet, dry them at once. Do not try to keep going. Also dry your clothing well each night.

Altitude Sickness (Mountain Sickness)

To some degree, all who travel abruptly to a higher altitude without acclimating, are affected by some of the symptoms of mountain sickness. In its mild states, the condition is marked by headache and difficulty sleeping. In the high country this is common during the first night at high altitude. Loss of appetite, drowsiness, mild nausea and shortness of breath are also common. These symptoms may increase in severity leading to vomiting, violent headaches, vertigo and unconsciousness. Humans can, given time, acclimate up to an altitude of about 18,000 feet. Beyond an altitude of 20,000 feet the body begins to deteriorate. The symptoms of altitude sickness may affect some persons as low as 6,000 feet, while others are comfortable at 15,000 feet. There is no hard fast rule.

The symptoms have always been attributed to lack of oxygen at higher altitudes, aggravated by heavy exertion, smoking, and drinking alcohol. Some recent research also seems to indicate a connection between a disruption of the acid/base balance in the body and altitude sickness. It was noted that approximately 90 percent of all mountain climbers had a shift to a more acid urine after several hours of climbing. If there is a connection between altitude sickness and acidosis, it would certainly seem logical. Both have nearly the same symptoms. A shift to an acid ph of the body fluids can result from impaired breathing in pathologic conditions. Certainly it might follow that the sudden reduction in oxygen inhaled at higher altitudes has the same effect. Additionally, muscular activity produces lactic acid as a waste product. This could further acidify the blood. A reduction of urine output, which often accompanies sweating, causes the ph to drop. All of these factors taken together would certainly build a good case for an acidosis/altitude sickness link.

The way to maintain the normal ph of body fluids is to have a fluid intake adequate to keep the kidneys flushed out. A urine output of about one quart every 24 hours would be adequate for this purpose. So, drink extra amounts of water, both during ascents and for several days beforehand. Reduce the intake of foods which cause an acid reaction in the body. These include meat, cheese, eggs, bread, noodles, peanuts, walnuts and corn, and fruits such as cranberries, plums and prunes. Foods which raise the ph in the body are: vegetables, jam, jellies, honey, milk, molasses, almonds, coconut and chestnuts. Neutral foods include plain candy, butter, cooking oil, syrups, and most other starches. Beyond this, the use of an antacid tablet such as Rolaids would be most beneficial during a climb.

If these measures prove effective they will be the first breakthrough in preventing a condition that is otherwise treated symptommatically, i.e., aspirin for headache, or with oxygen and evacuation to a lower altitude.

Pulmonary Edema

Until quite recently the existence of this condition was unknown, and many earlier cases in which climbers were reported to have died of pneumonia were actually caused by pulmonary edema. The condition affects younger climbers — especially males under 19; persons over 35 are rarely affected. Another group which seems susceptible are residents of high altitudes who visit lower altidudes for a few weeks, then return home. The disorder occurs when a susceptible person travels from a low-lying area to altitudes over 9,000 feet in the matter of a day or two. The condition is simply an accumulation of fluid in the lungs. Symptoms develop in 6 to 36 hours after arrival and consist of shortness of breath, weakness, coughing, and a tight feeling in the chest. Occasionally, loss of appetite, nausea and vomiting are also present. The cough is extremely irritating and constant, soon becoming productive of frothy white or pink sputum. The pulse becomes rapid (120 to 160), while respiration becomes rapid (20 to 40) and labored. Skin becomes pale or blue; body temperature is only slightly raised; and the mucous membranes do not show signs of inflammation. Coma and death may result within a few hours from suffocation or heart failure. The only treatment is to administer oxygen and quickly evacuate to a lower altitude. Breathing will be easier in the sitting position and complete rest is mandatory.

Thrombophlebitis

This is a serious vascular disorder which produces clotting of the blood in the leg veins. Most commonly a complication of surgery, it also has been diagnosed among mountaineers. While not a major factor for the Nordic skiier, the conditions which favor clotting are present and could be a factor for a person in whom exists a high risk of clotting. Dehydration from inadequate fluid intake thickens blood. Low temperatures decrease blood flow to the limbs, as does inactivity—such as experienced in a snowbound party which must remain in a cramped tent. At high altitudes the body releases an extra number of red blood cells into the circulation to make up for the loss of oxygen. But this also thickens the blood.

The most common symptoms of thrombophlebitis are pain in the calf, behind the knee and in the inner thigh. The pain often comes on suddenly and is aggravated by walking. Swelling of the affected leg usually occurs and the leg may be pale. This condition is a serious medical problem and should be carefully differentiated from muscle cramps in the legs. (See discussion of muscle cramps.) If the clot should break loose and enter the heart or lung it is a life-threatening problem. For this reason, if you believe a person has a clot, he should not walk under any conditions and should be evacuated.

Skin Care

Now that we have covered some of the really terrible things that can happen to you in the mountains, it seems appropriate to discuss some of the common-sense items that can make or break a trip. The skin is a very important and sensitive area of the body and certainly deserves special care when you are out in the back country. You should wear comfortable, well-fitting clothes that will not rub or chafe the skin. Control your body temperature so that you do not perspire more than absolutely necessary. Underclothing should be kept clean and dry and you should always have a fresh change of socks. Toenails should be clipped, especially for cross-country skiers. The foot action in this mode of travel tends to jam the foot into the boot and can cause you to lose your toenails if they are not kept quite short. Handling cold equipment with bare hands can cause a bad frost burn. This is best prevented by carrying a pair of glove liners and using them when fine work is called for. Also it is a good idea to wash up at night before you crawl into your sleeping bag. This will allow the skin sufficient time to replenish natural oils that help ward off wind or sunburn. It doesn't hurt the sleeping bag either. Liberal use of suntan lotion and lip gloss is also necessary, as is wearing protective clothing.

Blisters

Avoid them! Wear proper-fitting boots and socks, and do not allow your feet to become too warm or damp. If you tend to blister, apply molefoam to potential blister areas before you leave camp. At the first sign of burning, stop and take your boot off, dry your foot and apply molefoam. *Do not break blisters* unless they are large and ready to break by themselves. If you must break a blister, wash the area and use an antiseptic. Lance at the edge of the blister with a sterilized pin and cover it to protect from infection.

Dehydration (Loss of Fluids)

At high altitude you breathe more heavily and are apt to sweat profusely. Hence, you lose an unusual amount of water over a relatively short period of time. This alone can make you feel sick and weak. Don't guzzle a lot of water at once; take frequent sips and an occasional salt tablet. You will find you feel a lot better.

Hypoglycemia (Low Blood Sugar)

Cross-country skiers and mountain climbers burn an enormous amount of calories in a very short time. This is no time to be on a diet, because if your blood sugar gets low you may get a little funny in the head. You can't think straight; you become tired

A first-aid sled can be built from two pairs of skis.

and weakened; and your temper gets short. Your energy level drops and you could be setting yourself up for an attack of hypothermia. It's best to carry and suck on some hard candy. Honey drops work especially well — chocolate is fatty and hard to digest.

Heat Exhaustion

Heat exhaustion may seem out of place in a discussion of winter mountaineering medical problems. However, it can get very hot on snow fields in the spring. The radiation of infrared light from the snow and the heat of spring sunshine can combine to produce temperatures in the 90's.

I have personally come upon at least one mountaineer being treated for hypohermia by his well-intended companions who had read of the condition in a forestry service pamphlet. He was however, suffering from heat exhaustion, the exact opposite condition of hypothermia! The victim was in a state of collapse in the middle of a snow field. It was a bright sunny day with an air temperature of about 80°F. There was no wind and the climber was going uphill with a heavy pack.

Unfortunately, his companions saw only the snow and had only the limited information in the pamphlet. As a result they treated him for the wrong condition. This brings up a good argument for adequate first-aid training, common sense and a logical approach in diagnosing *before* rendering first aid.

Heat exhaustion symptoms are the result of exposure to excessive heat. Each of us responds differently to a given amount of heat. Therefore, there is no way of telling how much or how long such exposure need be. Heat exhaustion may even affect persons in excellent physical condition.

It is caused by extended periods of physical exertion in excessive heat. The blood vessels in the skin become so dilated in an attempt to cool the skin that the blood pools in the skin. This reduces the blood supply for the brain and other vital organs. Dehydration and salt deficiencies also can lead to heat exhaustion.

The victim is listless, fearful, may be semicomatose or, in severe cases, unconscious. The skin is cold and clammy; perspiration is profuse; and the victim appears very ill. Before the victim reaches this state he may develop weakness, dizziness, vertigo, headache, blurred vision, irritability and muscular cramps. If these symptoms appear, start treatment before things get worse. Treatment consists of cooling the victim and giving him water and salt tablets. Recovery is usually very rapid. However, if someone contracts heat exhaustion, he should exert extra caution with exposure to high temperature for several months afterward.

Physical Exhaustion

Exhaustion is a problem encountered by poorly conditioned travelers or those who simply bite off more than they can chew: In fact, it's probably the most common problem encountered on any trail. *Never* push yourself or any member of your party to a point of excessive fatigue. Doing so can only lead to accidents. When overly tired, you experience loss of willpower, confusion and poor judgement. In addition to such mental disaster goes muscle weakness, loss of coordination and muscle cramps. A person in this condition is an accident looking for a place to happen! Also there is increased susceptibility to hypothermia, heat exhaustion, altitude sickness, a cold or the flu. Keep goals and set a pace that is within the ability range of the entire party, and take frequent rest stops. Above all stay *warm, dry* and *well fed.*

Evacuation of Injured

In back country accident situations, where help is miles away or a great deal of time may be involved in removing the injured, proper diagnosis is very important. *If there is any doubt, treat for the worst condition.* With most injuries the victim can be brought out under his own power or with a little help. If it is necessary to ski an injured person out, remember to take your time and be patient and understanding. You will do far better with encouragement and a positive attitude than all the bullying in the world. Be supportive and kind but firm. And remain in control: the injured person will be alright if he just keeps going.

You should not try to ski out those with possible internal injuries, hemorrhages that cannot be stopped, fractures to the lower extemities, or spinal or head injuries. Also if the victim is suffering from shock or has lost consciousness, attempts at evacuation will be difficult. But in instances where there is no threat of further injury, the victim can be encouraged to come out under his own steam.

Someone with broken ribs, for example, could ski for miles without much difficulty. Since a fall would be both hazardous and painful, careful route selection and adequate support are necessary. The same might apply to someone with a splinted broken arm, a supported sprained ankle or a severe cut that has been dressed and is no longer bleeding. These are injuries for which, if you were in town, a person might be taken to the emergency room at the local hospital. But out in the back country you're just going to have to grit your teeth and make do.

It may sound a bit hard-nosed, but if you wish to go out into the back country you can't expect the National Ski Patrol to come riding over the nearest hill to carry you to a nice, heated first-aid room at the first sign of a twisted knee.

For the badly injured, where some form of evacuation is necessary, the last thing you want to do is carry the victim in a makeshift stretcher. This may become necessary, and if it does you'd best be prepared to do it. But try everything else first. In some regions of the country caches of first-aid equipment are available. Some of these include a toboggan. If you venture out in areas where such caches are located be sure you determine their location. In any case, before you leave for the back country, you must find out what local aid is available and where and how to reach it.

Many of us do not have a high regard for snowmobiles. But after using one to evacuate someone who is badly hurt, you may get down and kiss its headlight.

Should it become necessary to make and use a stretcher or toboggan in the back country, it can be done using two pairs of skis. It will be makeshift at best but it will do. Use the following procedures:

> Lay out two pair of skis parallel so that they are about 24 inches across from the outer edges.

> Cut three lenghts of disaster wood (green or live sticks 1 to 1½ inches in diameter) about three feet long. Lay these across the tops of the skis, one at the front just behind the shovel, one just in front of the binding, and one at the tail.

> Lash these cross-poles tightly to the skis. Cotton cord works well and will not stretch when wet. Cut six-foot lengths and wrap it very tightly. Do not fasten the cord to either the wood or the ski, but tie the two ends together when the wrapping is done. Place the knot on top of the pole, never under the ski. Wax the cord heavily with ski wax.

> Attach cross-braces using nylon cord. A loop is placed around the end of the center cross-pole in the center of the cord. Either end of the cord is then attached to the opposite front and rear cross-poles. A trucker's knot is used to pull this as tight as possible. Repeat using the opposite ends of the cross-poles.

This device can be used as a stretcher with the injured lashed to the bottom of the skis and carried by up to six persons. The ends of the cross-poles are used as handles. If you use this device as a toboggan, the injured should be placed on top of the skis and a pull rope attached to the middle and front cross-poles. Pine boughs may be laid across the toboggan with the branches pointing backward for additional padding and insulation. In either case, an insolite pad can also be placed under the injured and protective clothing or tarps used to cover him.

First-Aid Equipment

The question of what to carry for first-aid equipment has a variety of answers. A short day trip in familar woodland near your home or cabin may require only minimal gear. While larger groups on extended trips into remote areas will have to carry rather extensive equipment—as exposure to injury increases and availability of help decreases.

You must size up your situation to determine what to carry on any given trip. The following suggestions are for two possible types of trips. The first is a day trip with several skiers taking a tour through easy country, not venturing more than a mile or two from the road. The second is a group traveling two to three days into a wilderness area. In either case, these items are only suggestions which you will probably have to adopt your list in order to cover any special problems that might be encountered.

Day Trip First-Aid Pack

Suntan lotion and chapstick
Antiseptic first-aid cream
Molefoam
Triangular bandages (3)
Bandaids (a few assorted sizes)
Elastic bandage (3-inch)
Sterile gauze pads (4 by 4)
Adhesive tape (roll of 2-inch)
Aspirin or other pain medication
Salt tablets and sugar (hard candy)

Overnight Back Country First-Aid Pack

Suntan lotion and chapstick—glacier cream in high
mountains
Antiseptic cream
Molefoam
Triangular bandages (4 to 6)
Bandaids (complete assortment, including butter-
flies)
Elastic bandages (one 3-inch and one 4-inch)
Sterile gauze pads (2 by 2, 4 by 4, 6 by 6)
Adhesive tape (roll of 3-inch)
Rolled gauze bandages (4 to 6)
Wire splint (¼- inch wire screen, 36 by 18 inches)
Aspirin, plus stronger pain medication if practical

Antacid tablets
Salt tablets and sugar (hard candy)
Tweezers
Magnifying glass (one, on a compass will do)
Q-tips

Other items talked about previously, such as a good knife, are also essential to first aid. In addition, in mountaineering or any winter situation, something which can be used to construct a shelter and start a fire are part of your first-aid gear and should never be left out.

First aid in the mountains means using everything you have and then inventing more. It means keeping the injured alive— possibly through a long and cold night. It can also mean gritting your teeth and moving out when it would be a lot easier to sit in the snow and cry.

Related Reading

Darvill, Fred T. Jr. *Mountaineering Medicine.* Skasit
    Mountain Rescue Unit, Mt. Vernon, WA, 1969
Lathrop, Theodore, M.D. *Hypothermia: Killer of the
    Unprepared.* Magamas, Portland, OR, 1972
MacInnes, Hamish; *International Mountain Rescue
    Handbook.* Charles Scribner's Sons, New York,
    1973
Starkov, P. *The Problem of Acute Hypothermia.*
    Pergamon Press, New York, 1960
Washburn, Bradford, *Frostbite, What It Is, How To
    Prevent It.* Emergency Treatment Museaum of
    Science, Boston MA, 1970
Wilderson, J. P. MD, *Medicine for Mountaineering.*
    The Mountaineers, Seattle, WA, 1973
The Committee on Injuries American Academy of
    Orthopedic Surgeons, *Emergency Care and
    Transportation of the Sick and Injured* Ameri-
    can Academy of Orthopedic Surgeons, Chica-
    go, IL,1971
The American National Red Cross, *Advanced First-
    Aid and Emergency Care.* Doubleday & Compa-
    ny, Inc. Garden City, NY, 1973

8

Survival

When all is said and done, surviving a disaster is a matter of mental attitude. Many studies have been made of groups that have survived shipwrecks, plane crashes, blizzards, mountaineering accidents and other occurences that have placed humans in unexpected situations. And all of these studies bear out one factor: It is the individual who keeps calm and figures out the best course of action and then continues on that course, even beyond the supposed limits of human effort, who makes it. In larger groups, the group that survives is the one in which a member of the party steps out and assumes strong leadership. Groups with such leadership function as a team with singular purpose. They conserve effort, stick together and support one another. Without good leadership, each person is apt to strike out on his own and flounder in the effort. These groups are marked by bodies found strung out across a wide area.

If you are in a group when disaster strikes, establish strong military discipline, elect or appoint the best leader, and then follow him. If alone, work out the problem in your mind and then keep going. *The ability to keep going is only limited by a state of unconsciousness and the lack of will to go on.*

Men with both legs broken have been known to crawl on their stomachs for hundreds of miles to get help. People with serious injuries have nursed themselves back to health and traveled miles back to civilization. And others have gone for weeks without food or days without water and yet never given up.

The newspapers are full of accounts of young, healthy individuals who become confused and lost, dying only a few yards off the road. In some cases these are college boys who died as a result of a fraternity initiation prank or Boy Scouts who became lost on a weekend outing. Also, there have been stories of elderly persons freezing to death in their own homes, after the utilities had been turned off. In every one of these tales of tragedy, the victims had one thing in common — they simply lay down and gave up. In so doing, they signed their own death certificates.

By refusing to just give up and die, you'll be surprised what you can accomplish. There are, however, some basic requirements to life that must be considered—including air, water, shelter, food and, in most cases, transportation.

Air

Without a supply of fresh air, a human usually loses consciousness in about five minutes and dies in less than 10 minutes. In avalanche situations, the snow is somewhat porous and survival time may be extended if the victim has an air pocket or is obtaining air from the snow. But no matter how large the air pocket, the warm exhaled air soon melts the walls and they ice over, preventing further air from entering the pocket. This is also true of snow caves, which breathe at first, but soon become iced over. Plastic or coated nylon tents do not breathe either; so on a cold night when you are tempted to close up the tent for warmth, remember what would happen if you placed a plastic bag over your head and went to sleep.

Fumes from cook stoves are the other great killers in winter shelters. The insidious buildup of lethal carbon monoxide will lull the senses, with the victim falling asleep, never to awaken again. Therefore, in shelters of any kind you must always have two vents; one for the intake of fresh air and other to exhaust smoke and fumes.

Water

Without a supply of water, survival times vary considerably, depending primarily on how fast your body is losing water. On a hot desert, death may occur within one day. But in cold climates, where the water loss by perspiration is far less, the survival time will be extended. In the case of the cross-country skier, finding water should not present too great a problem, as there is usually plenty of ice and snow at hand.

Of course, the easiest source is stream water or water lying under pond ice. But be careful when walking on ice. If you fall through the ice you are at once in great danger. Also, *keep off ponds which are created behind dams.* Very often (sometimes a power company does it intentionally) the water level is lowered after the lake has frozen over. This leaves a large air space under a dome of ice. Without the water to hold the weight of the ice, it will break at the drop of a hat. You could find yourself in ice cold water several feet below a layer of ice, a death trap if there ever was one. If you fall into the water in the winter, the result is instant hypothermia; so exercise great caution anywhere around streams, ponds and lakes.

Another suggestion is to check out the source of the water. It is just as important not to drink polluted water in the winter as it is in the summer. You might also look below ledges where the sun is shining on the rocks. The sun melts the snow causing water to drip, forming either icicles or small rivulets of water which run down the rock. In addition, a dark colored plastic bag will generate enough heat to melt snow, if it is hung up in the sun. And water dripping off trees may have a bitter taste but is usually drinkable.

One kind of snow to be avoided is colored snow. We need not mention yellow snow. However, large patches of red snow may be visible, especially in the spring. This is caused by an algae growing in the snow. Under some conditions, this same algae may appear green. However, the end result of eating the snow or drinking water melted from it are the same: First, it tastes slightly like watermelon; second, it will produce one of the wildest cases of diarrhea you will ever encounter.

Food

Spending a great deal of time and effort trying to find a source of food is usually wasteful. People can live a long time without food. A five-day fast, if you are careful and do not overexert will not be much fun, but should have no ill effects. Remember to compare the amount of energy required to obtain the food versus the amount of energy to be derived from the food. In woodland areas covered by snow there are generally no edible plants. One possible exception are pine needles, which can be used to make a tea that is bitter but does furnish warmth and a small amount of energy.

If there are plenty of rabbit or other small game tracks about, you might try setting up a snare or dead fall. But as a general rule, this is not neccessary because you are not probably far from help. By rationing both food and energy, you can make it out of the wilderness. In planning any trip, however, toss in a few extra rations as a safety margin, and hope you will never have to use them. As a psychological trick on yourself, bring something you really hate. That way you will not be tempted to eat it the first time you get hungry and will save the food until it's really needed.

Another precaution is never eat all of your lunch. Even when things have gone well and there has been no need for emergency rations, these leftovers can serve as a quick pick-me-up when you get back to the trailhead.

Shelters

Whenever you travel in the back country always keep an eye out for a possible emergency shelter. It can be a cave, windfall, natural snow cave, cabin, fire lookout, forestry service camp or supply shed. Keep anything you find in mind and remember its location. Several such shelters might be required over a period of a long evacuation, so plan your routes accordingly. In the event that no ready-made shelter is at hand and you must construct a shelter, allow lots of time to do the job right. If setting up a tent in the dark is hard, making an improvised shelter is 10 times harder. First rule: Get below the snowline. Snow usually stays about 32°F, and with your body heat to warm the air and no wind to conduct warm air way from you, the inside of a snow house can get well above the freezing level—which is one reason they tend to drip. If it gets warm and starts to rain, they also leak like a sieve. Doming the ceiling, so that the water will run down the sides, is a possible solution. Second rule: Make the job as simple as possible. Use any natural aid available, i.e., a windfall or brush pile. The branches will add a lot of support.

If the snow is hard and heavily packed, tunneling into a drift may work. But if it is wet and packs easily, rolling large snowballs and using them to build an igloo may be the best move. Also, glacial or hard-packed snow can be cut into blocks to construct a block house. If you are in deep, fresh powder snow that is very dry, lots of luck!

Once inside your shelter, remove anything metallic which could conduct heat away from your body. This would include earrings, glasses, watches, rings, crampons or any other metallic object. Loosen all clothing but keep it closed tight to prevent air leaks. Take your arms out of the jacket sleeves and turn the

A windfall shelter

Tree shelter

sleeves inside out, crossing them behind you. Then fold your arms across your chest with your hands in your armpits. This gives your back the extra warmth of the crossed sleeves and keeps your arms and hands close to your body for warmth. Remember, too, that an extra pair of socks can double as mittens and vice versa. You can also use the old hobo trick and pack your clothes with any extra dry clothing available; even wadded up paper or dry wood pulp will create insulation.

Line your shelter with bark off trees or pine boughs to keep you off the snow. This step should only be taken in real emergency cases, as it does mess up the ecology. In the shelter, sit on your pack to get as much insulation between you and the snow as possible. Wriggle around inside your clothes to help circulation and to keep you warm. Even wearing your wool shirt right next to the skin and then giving an occasional wriggle will get the circulation going in the skin.

Next, after all possible layers of insulation have been constructed and, if possible, a fire is going, it helps to think about being warm. Do not tell yourself how darn cold you are; instead, keep a strong mental image of a hot day at the beach or of sitting too close to a roaring fire. Keeping these thoughts in your mind actually triggers a response in the body to increase circulation and thereby warm you. If you are with someone else, talk about warm summer things and keep yourselves thinking about how warm you are. Negative thoughts in times of real trouble can be a greater enemy than the worst that the elements can throw at you.

Types of Shelters

There are several different kinds of simple shelters which can be adapted for use in emergency conditions or, if you are careful of the ecology and do not mind the work, can be built for regular camping. The one to avoid is a tarp haphazardly tied to your skis or trees; it is too vulnerable to wind and weather.

In constructing any shelter in the snow, especially where digging is required, be sure to wear protective clothing. You can become increasingly wet and get a lot of snow down your neck if you are not properly dressed and careful. Rain pants and a waterproof parka with a hood are very important.

Snow Pit. The simplest shelter to construct is a snow pit. Dig straight down, stopping just before you reach ground level. Put some form of cross brace over the top and lay a tarp over this.

Lean-to

Then cover the tarp with a layer of snow to prevent it from blowing away. By digging an inclined tunnel for an entrance you have produced a very workable shelter.

Brush Pile Shelter. Finding a windfall or brush pile with snow piled over the top may give you an almost ready-made snow cave. Some extra digging and patching of holes will finish the job.

Pine Bough Shelter. At the base of tall conifer trees there is often a sizable snow pit ready-made. In deep snow the lower limbs become weighted with snow and sag to the ground. Beneath the tree, against the trunk, is where you will find the cave. Again, some extra digging and filling will put it in order.

Overhanging Ledges. An overhanging ledge with a little cave is also a good place to seek shelter. Pile some brush in front of the overhang and add a tarp for windproofing. One word of caution: Rocks can be far colder than snow and often conduct heat away from the body.

Lean-To. In reasonably protected areas a three-sided lean-to makes an excellent shelter. Place long poles against two adjacent trees or the top of a large rock. Next lash cross members to the poles, lay a tarp on top, and pile snow onto the tarp and at the ends of the lean-to. Add a good fire reflector in front of the lean-to to bounce heat back under the overhang and you will have a very cozy shelter. It suffers from exposure to wind and storms, but on quiet nights it is warm.

The Igloo. Probably the hardest shelter to build, the igloo requires some practice and skill, but if properly constructed it makes an excellent shelter. You should have some form of snow saw or cutting tool to do the job right. Blocks of snow are cut with the ice saw so that they are tapered on each surface toward the face which will be the inner wall. The blocks are then placed in a circle with subsequent levels being added to produce a dome. A final key block will support the dome. With some loose snow packed into the chinks, the structure will freeze solid.

Snow Cave. The time-honored snow cave is a warm and comfortable shelter if constructed properly. Some wilderness experts rate the snow cave as the most desirable of all winter shelters, even better than tents. Again, they do require skill and practice for proper construction. Best done in old, well-packed snow, you must first find a suitable pile of snow and start a horizontal tunnel. Once in far enough to support the front wall, enlarge the cave to the desired dimensions. Always leave the ceiling dome shaped, as this allows water to run off and prevents dripping. Then, too, a dome creates a structurally strong ceiling.

In constructing any shelter, always leave adequate ventilation. If you cap the entrance against wind, leave a double air hole and make sure the holes do not become plugged during the night. Also, be careful when building a fire outside the entrance of a shelter. You might feel safer with the fire outside, believing the fumes would not build up in your shelter. But in a poorly ventilated shelter, you could burn off the oxygen at the entrance and allow a build up of CO_2 within the shelter. While less deadly than carbon monoxide, carbon dioxide can still kill you.

Fire

Man's single greatest tool, fire, can warm and dry you and give you comfort against the night and light against the darkness. It or its smoke may serve as a beacon to rescuers. Hence, whenever possible, in cases of disaster, build a good fire. Use a proper windbreak and ration the firewood carefully.

Fires are best started by using matches or a cigarette lighter. Rubbing two sticks together, unless they are good and hard and you are both patient and experienced, will only be a waste of time and effort. An alternate method of starting a fire, which does work, is to use a burning glass: Focus the sun's rays through a magnfying glass onto a piece of paper or other tinder. Some compasses have small magnifying lenses built into them. Or, if you have a camera with you, open the back and remove the film; then focus the sun through the front of the lens out the back of the camera onto the tinder. Remember you must hold the shutter open, as though you were taking a time exposure, in order for this to work.

Gather your fuel carefully before you try to start the fire. There are a number of first-class fire-starting compounds on the market, and bringing some along is a good camping practice. Lacking these, a bit of candle wax or ski wax will help. Also, a few scraps of paper or the lint from the bottoms of your pockets can be useful. Dry pine needles, pine cones, birch bark, and dry leaves also work well as tinder. Or you can cut a stick into many paper-thin shavings, leaving the base of each shaving attached to the stick. The shavings curl outward, making an easily ignited fire stick.

Igloo

Snow cave

You can get the maximum heat from a fire by using a heat re-flector. Building a fire against a large rock will bounce the heat off the rock or other surface and back toward the fire. Putting a second reflector behind you will cause the heat to be bounced back and forth, warming the area very well. Again, a plug for ecology—remember the rock and fire trick is discussed under survival. Fire-scarred rocks do not add to the beauty of the countryside. Another life-saving, ecology-wrecking trick is to find a large, old, dead hollow tree. These old crags can be set afire quite readily by building a fire inside them. Once it gets going, you will have a fire which will burn several days and give out a great deal of warmth. It is also one heck of a signal beacon. However, this should only be tried in the winter, with a good snow cover, as there is little point in starting forest fires just to stay warm. This sort of fire also causes a ranger to do a pretty good burn, so only use it when it is really needed.

Travel

If you find yourself in a situation where you must travel in heavy snow, remember, you must travel *over*, not through the snow. One of the most totally exhausting experiences in the world is trying to wade through deep snow. You become cold, wet and tired almost at once. If your equipment has failed or a ski is bro-ken, repair it first, even if it means an éxtra day before you can move. If this is impossible, make a pair of snowshoes: Bend two sticks together and lash them at the ends. Then separate them in the middle with other branches and weave a lacework of cord to support your weight. Fashion a sling to hold your foot, walk carefully and pray a lot. If you find yourself in such a situation, remember that the snow is hardest around dawn. So try to travel early to prevent sinking in.

Lost

Should all your best route-finding efforts fail and for some rea-son you do lose your bearings and become lost, there are a few simple steps to remember.

First, panic is not helpful, but is a frequent result of the fear and confusion caused by being lost. Even if they don't panic, many people get their ego involved—they don't want to admit even to themselves that they're lost. Little else can make one feel more ridiculous than not knowing where he is or how to get to where he wants to be.

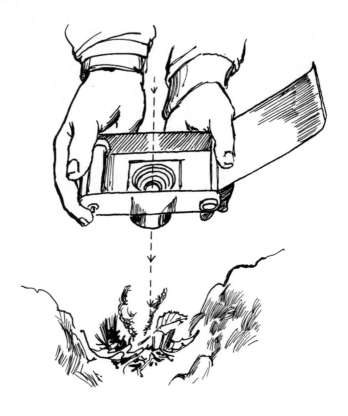

A fire can be started with a camera if matches or a cigarette lighter are not available.

It's important to stop as soon as you find yourself in a situation where you are unsure of your direction or location. Before continuing, figure things out and initiate a plan of action. Far too often a person feels that if he just keeps going, sooner or later he will come out on familiar ground. Then everything will be all right and no one will know he was lost. Instead, what often happens is that he keeps going all right, but in the wrong direction. He gets completely twisted around and walks in circles; ends up miles away or in the middle of the worst mess of slash brush in that or any adjoining county.

If you are unable to work out your location with a map and compass, then a quick search should be started. First, mark the point where you are presently standing; mark it well, so you may return to it if necessary. Then start a series of short probes, extending like the spokes of a wheel from your base. Pick the most logical direction first and travel in a straight line for a set distance. Use a compass if at all possible. But if you do not have a compass, take a bearing on a landmark and go to it. Always mark your trail and return to your base over the exact same route if the probe has not been successful. Starting from your original position, pick a new direction and travel the exact same distance in that direction, repeating the process until you come out on familiar ground.

If done with care this wagon-wheel method usually works. The distance traveled on each probe can be as far as you feel practical. It may be anywhere from 200 to 300 yards; or at other times, a distance of a mile might be required. But no matter how far you go, when you get to the limit of the probe return to the original starting point. *Never get to the end of a probe and start out on a new heading.* If you do, you will just end up wandering and could travel many miles from where a search party will be looking for you.

There are many landmarks that will aid you in locating civilization. Much of the country is crisscrossed by fence lines and power lines. Following either of these will eventually lead you out to a road. But in parts of the western United States, if you pick the wrong direction to travel, this could be a long trip. Those power lines and ranch fences can go for miles. If you have not come out after what you consider a reasonable distance, it is best to mark the point and go back in the other direction instead of just plodding along. In any case if you should find a power line, it is well to stick with it; search parties tend to check these areas very closely.

Logging or fire roads can be long twisting paths; on occasion they form a maze that will take days of wandering to sort out. However, where there is a road, there is always a way out. So stick to the road and use the pattern of marking the route and returning to a given point if your travel along a reasonable distance does not yield a way home. Remember, logging roads are like the branches of a tree—smaller roads lead into larger ones and finally to a main heavily traveled road out of the area. Hence, when traveling a small road, look for a larger or more heavily traveled road.

The old story about heading down a stream until you come out of the woods works in many cases. This method does have its faults and caution should be used before you strike off downstream. In the eastern United States, streams can end up in swamps, and they are places to stay out of at all costs. If you come across a swamp, go around. *Never cross a swamp.* Even in the winter they are filled with brush piles, tanglefoot and pot holes, all of which tend to be very tiring to the weary traveler.

In the north woods, streams can flow into lakes and into other streams. They can wander for miles, so unless you are acquainted with the country, have some second thoughts before striking out along a wandering stream.

Out in the western states, streams have a bad habit of ending up in the bottoms of canyons. Such canyons not only run for miles but tend to get deeper the farther they go. Getting up out of one can be a day's job in itself. Again, knowing the country and the direction of major streams in the area before you leave the road will tell you whether you should follow the brook. However, people who take time to study the landscape and maps before they leave on a trip are not the ones who usually get lost.

If you have looked in all directions and still not found your way, return to your original point, or as close to it as possible, set up camp and wait for help. Further wandering will only take you away from the area where search parties should be looking.

At this point your whistle becomes vital. If you are with others, it should have been used to re-establish contact on your probes. However, if you must wait out rescue, remember that the human voice does not carry well and soon becomes hoarse and tired from continued calls. But, a good police whistle can be heard at great distances and does not blend in with other natural sounds. It also takes less energy to use. However, even when blasting away on a whistle, remember that sound is effected by many things. Trees and snow, especially new-fallen snow, absorb a great deal of sound. Remember how quiet the woods are after a new snow?

If signaling for help, get out in the open or on a high rock, both to make yourself more visible and to allow the sound to carry as far as possible. Move away from running water as this will mask the sound. There is little you can do about the wind except to remember that sound will be carried farther downwind and will not be heard at any distance upwind.

A standard system of signals is necessary to avoid confusion. This is true whether you are using a light at night, a signal mirror, or a whistle. The most common accepted usage is:

Three—*Help, come to me.*
Two—*Hold position, or return to base.*
One—*Answer my call.*

Thus, searchers would use a single call, while the lost individual would use three. This avoids confusion and allows different searchers to zero in on the person needing help.

Cross-country racer

Many local colleges and adult education programs offer pre-ski conditioning classes.

Cross-country skiing can be as mild as a walk in the park on a summer day; or it can be one of the most grueling outdoor sports known to man.

Appendix

Don't Get Snowed was written at the request of the United States Ski Association (USSA) Ski Touring and Mountaineering Committee for use in conjunction with the USSA Ski Touring Patch (White Diamond) and Ski Mountaineering Patch (Green Diamond) courses.

The Diamond courses are major parts of USSA's program of public education in superior skiing skills and ski safety. The courses, which are taught by USSA volunteers and affiliated groups, are offered annually in many parts of the country. Simply stated, the purpose of the courses is to teach intermediate skiers technical information on safety in the back country, distinguishing the knowledgable skier from the mere athlete.

A typical course, which starts in January, includes six to 10 lectures, meeting once a week for three hours. In addition, two field trips are included in each course. The first trip is six to eight hours long, but the second trip is a major field exercise, intended to provide practical experience in as much of the course material as possible. This second trip is 54 hours long, involving at least two nights out. The field trips provide the distinction between the Green and White Diamond programs. The Green Diamond is awarded after completion of Ski Mountaineering field trips undertaken in terrain of high relief, while the White Diamond is awarded for Ski Touring field trips in terrain of more moderate relief.

A skier who completes either of the Diamond courses should acquire a knowledge of mountain winter hazards and the precautions to take in traversing mountainous or primitive terrain in winter conditions. He will be taught to prepare for travel on skis, including the basics of food, warmth, shelter and route finding. Course participants will be required to demonstrate broad knowledge of the basics of winter survival, including food, clothing, shelter, and equipment, orientation and route selection and camp and travel under winter conditions in the wild. An effort will be made to develop in each person sufficient leadership capability, ability to care for an accident victim and to be a safe leader of club ski touring or ski mountaineering trips. Diamond Award holders are expected to inform the public about mountain winter safety and procedures necessary to avoid the hazards of this sport. Patch holders are also expected to have achieved some proficiency in ski touring or ski mountaineering skills.

Enrollment in the classroom sessions of the course is open to everyone, but advanced intermediate skiing ability is required for the field trips. Course participants may be requested to postpone participation in the second field trip if their skiing skills appear inadequate during the first trip. All participants *must* have become USSA members and have acquired an American Red Cross First-Aid card of some type before the second field trip.

The course had its origins shortly before World War II, in preparation for conflict. In 1940, the Board of Directors of the National Ski Association (as USSA was then called) voted to establish a nationwide ski mountaineering training course. The NSA ski mountaineering course helped prepare many skiers for the rigors of life in the 10th Mountain Division and provided the Army with an invaluable model for their training programs.

After the war, the NSA continued to offer the course as a recreational program for its members, until the early 1950's, when the present patch design and course name were adopted. During the 1960's, Alpine skiing's popularity caused the demand for the Nordic program to decline substantially. However, Leo Hoefer and his associates in the ski patrol used the Diamond program concepts and ideas in developing the National Ski Patrol Ski Mountaineering Patch training programs.

The U.S. ski scene started to change in the early 1970's, with a dramatic increase in interest in ski touring and ski mountaineering. The USSA pledged to develop a full range of Nordic Recreation programs equal in value to its Alpine programs, and the decision was made to give top priority to rejuvenating old programs, including the Diamond program. During the 1973-74 season, the White Diamond (ski touring) course was added, an annual instructors clinic was established to train program leaders and create program uniformity and it was decided to commission a new manual for the course.

Mike Riley was asked to undertake the task of preparing this new manual. The first draft of *Don't Get Snowed* was made available in 1977 and until recently was used in some Diamond programs. The present edition incorporates criticisms and improvements from instructors around the country.

The Diamond program has grown substantially in recent years, and courses are now offered in many parts of the country. However, there are still some areas where courses are not available. USSA is still actively seeking local clubs, universities and other groups to give courses under USSA sanction. Skiers seeking information about obtaining sanction for their program or information about when and where the course nearest them will be offered should write to the: United States Ski Association, 1726 Champa Street, Suite #300, Denver, CO 80202.

Gar Bering
Vice-President
Nordic Recreation
USSA

The United States Ski Association (USSA) is a non-profit volunteer service organization for skiers dedicated to improving the sport of skiing. The USSA works with industry and public agencies representing the individual skier's interests, seeks ways of making skiing less expensive, and operates a variety of recreational programs. The group also organizes and operates all amateur skiing events recognized by the U.S. Olympic Committee and the International Ski Federation, including all National Championships.

Discounts

The association's 100,000 members have access to discounts on guided tours, lessons, meals, lodging, European and domestic ski holidays, ski equipment, ski apparel, transportation, even automobile tires and batteries.

Touring Facility Advocate

USSA acts as a public advocate, lobbying for more and better touring facilities. Currently, the organization is working for more funding of touring trail construction, and to protect touring areas from abuse and snowmobile intrusion. Members are also working for more uniform trail signs, more packing of touring areas, and wider dissemination of safety information by public agencies.

USSA runs a Hut system in the Colorado Rockies, and is presently raising funds to build more elsewhere in the country' In addition, The Association's Trails Committee is working on ways to help local groups develop more trails.

Competitive Programs

In cross-country skiing, U.S. representatives in the Olympics and World Championships are selected on the basis of performance in amateur events sanctioned by USSA, and run by officials trained and certified in USSA programs. Members are eligible to obtain a personalized race card and a permanent racer history which establishes regional ranking by sex and age group.

Information Distributor

USSA and its regional divisions publish route guide books, Nordic ski events calendar, directories of retail services and a Ski Touring Trail planner. With the U.S. Forest Service, the group publishes a Winter Recreation Safety Guide. Beyond books, USSA assists in theformation of local clubs, Council Nordic programs and guided tours.

Group Insurance

Comprehensive ski-insurance programs are offered to USSA members. A special insurance program devised for the cross-country skier, includes Search and Rescue, Ski Guard ski accident coverage and Ski Theft.

Skiing Publications

Most of the association's regional divisions publish a newspaper, typically in ten monthly editions. These publications keep the skier up-to-date on local, national and international skiing news, including the latest information on legislation affecting skiing, USSA recreational and competitive programs.

The USSA Ski Tourer's Pledge[*]

I will protect the land and natural resources of the land on which I ski. I will make it my personal business to leave the land in such a condition that, except for the tracks of my skis upon the snow, no one will ever know that I was there. I will always treat the land gently so that I may return in the future and be welcomed as an old friend.

*Written 1971 by Leo Hannan, Chairman, USSA Ski Touring
 and Mountaineering Committee, 1971-72. Adopted as the
 official USSA Ski Tourer's Pledge, at the Annual Conven-
 tion, June, 1972, Portland, Oregon.

©USSA 1977

Don't Get Snowed has also been approved by the National Ski
Patrol System, Inc. (NSPS) for use as an official text in the organization's Ski Mountaineering training programs. NSPS mountaineering advisors and instructors have contributed many suggestions for the book.

General Related Reading

Brower, David, ed., *Manual of Ski Mountaineering.* 4th ed., Ballentine Books, New York, 1969

Manning, Harvey, ed. *Mountaineering, the Freedom of the Hills.* The Mountaineers, Seattle, WA

Steck, Allen and Lito Tejada-Flores, *Wilderness Skiing.* Sierra Club Books, 597 5th Ave., New York 10017

Blackshaw, Allen, *Mountaineering, From Hill Walking to Alpine Climbing.* Penguin Books, 1970

Baldwin, Edward R., *The Cross-Country Skiing Handbook.* Charles Scribner's Sons, New York, 1972

Bradford, Angier, *Skills for Taming the Wilds.* Pocket Books, New York, 1967

Brady, M. Michael, *Nordic Touring and Cross Country Skiing.* Port City Press, Inc., New York, 1971

Index